SpringerBriefs in Computer Science

Series Editors
Stan Zdonik
Shashi Shekhar
Jonathan Katz
Xindong Wu
Lakhmi C. Jain
David Padua
Xuemin (Sherman) Shen
Borko Furht
V.S. Subrahmanian
Martial Hebert
Katsushi Ikeuchi
Bruno Siciliano
Sushil Jajodia
Newton Lee

More information about this series at http://www.springer.com/series/10028

Aleksandar Čolić • Oge Marques
Borko Furht

Driver Drowsiness Detection

Systems and Solutions

 Springer

Aleksandar Čolić
Department of Computer & Electrical
  Engineering
Florida Atlantic University
Boca Raton, FL, USA

Oge Marques
Department of Computer & Electrical
  Engineering and Computer Science
Florida Atlantic University
Boca Raton, FL, USA

Borko Furht
Department of Computer Science &
  Engineering
Florida Atlantic University
Boca Raton, FL, USA

ISSN 2191-5768   ISSN 2191-5776 (electronic)
ISBN 978-3-319-11534-4   ISBN 978-3-319-11535-1 (eBook)
DOI 10.1007/978-3-319-11535-1
Springer Cham Heidelberg New York Dordrecht London

Library of Congress Control Number: 2014949174

Printed on acid-free paper

Springer is part of Springer Science+Business Media (www.springer.com)

To my beloved parents whose unconditional love and support know no bounds. – AČ

To Ingrid, for her unfailing support, love, and encouragement. – OM

Preface

This short book presents an overview of driver drowsiness detection systems and associated technologies and available solutions.

There is a substantial amount of evidence that suggests that driver drowsiness plays a significant role in road accidents, claiming the lives of thousands of people every year worldwide. This is a problem that needs to be seriously addressed. If vehicles become equipped with technology capable of detecting signs of driver drowsiness in a timely manner, many potential accidents will be prevented and many lives will be spared as a result.

In this monograph we define drowsiness and quantify its impact and significance, describe several different methods for measuring and detecting driver drowsiness, survey existing solutions, provide guidance on how they can be implemented, and discuss the associated technical challenges.

It is targeted at researchers and practitioners in the fields of engineering and computer science. It caters particularly to readers who want to develop their own methods and systems for driver drowsiness detection using computer vision, image processing, and machine learning techniques to detect driver drowsiness using behavioral cues (e.g., nodding of the head, yawning, or closing of the eyes for prolonged periods of time) and alert the driver accordingly.

We expect that the book will fulfill its goal of serving as a preliminary reference on the subject. Readers who want to deepen their understanding of specific topics will find more than a hundred references to additional sources of related information.

We would like to thank Susan Lagerstrom-Fife and her staff at Springer for their support throughout this project.

Boca Raton, FL, USA   Aleksandar Čolić
July 2014   Oge Marques
                                                                                        Borko Furht

Contents

Chapter 1
Introduction

This chapter provides an introduction to the topic of driver drowsiness detection. Through crash statistics and other related data, it demonstrates the importance and seriousness of the subject. Moreover, it introduces some of the terminology and concepts related to this topic.

1.1 The Problem of Driver Drowsiness

The interest in equipping vehicles with driver drowsiness detection systems has been motivated by alarming statistics, such as the 2013 World Health Organization report [15] stating that: 1.24 million people die on the road every year; approximately 6 % of all the accidents are caused by drivers driving in a drowsy state; and most of the accidents of this type result in fatalities.

Shocking statistics revealed by World Health Organization (WHO) in a 2009 report [14] showed that more than 1.2 million people die on roads around the world every year. Moreover, an additional 20–50 million individuals suffer non-fatal injuries. Such astonishing numbers have triggered community action. For example, the United Nations (UN) General Assembly dedicated the decade between 2011 and 2020 to be the *Decade of Action for Road Safety*. A recently published follow-up report by the WHO [15] showed that even though some progress has been made, the shocking figure of 1.24 million deaths caused by road accidents per year remains essentially the same. An analysis of the number of deaths by age range (Fig. 1.1) shows that almost 40 % are young people, below the age of 30.

A Report from the National Highway Traffic Safety Administration (NHTSA) from 1994 [6] provided statistics on how many accidents are caused by drowsy driving. An average annual total of 6.3 million police reported crashes occurred during the period between 1989 and 1993 in the United States. Of these, approximately 100,000 crashes per year (i.e., 1.6 % of 6.3 million) were identified with

© The Author(s) 2014
A. Čolić et al., *Driver Drowsiness Detection*, SpringerBriefs in Computer Science,
DOI 10.1007/978-3-319-11535-1_1

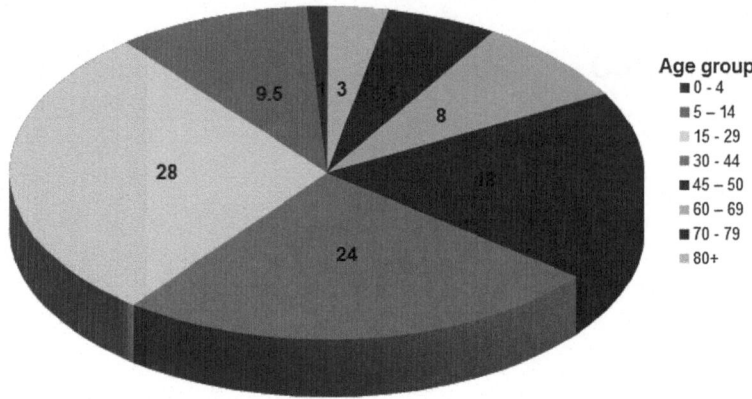

Fig. 1.1 Proportion of road traffic deaths by age range

drowsiness in the corresponding Police Crash Reports (PCR). Additionally, many other accident reports referred to "Drift-Out-Of-Lane" crashes, which might be related to drowsiness aspects as well. Approximately 71,000 of all drowsy-related crashes involved non-fatal injuries, whereas 1,357 drowsy-related fatal crashes resulted in 1,544 fatalities (3.6 % of all fatal crashes), as reported by the Fatality Analysis Reporting System (FARS). Nevertheless, many run-off-roadway crashes are not reported or cannot be verified by police, suggesting that the problem is much larger than previously estimated.

A significant number of surveys, studies and reports suggest that drowsiness is one of the biggest causes of road accidents. The US National Sleep Foundation (NSF) reported that 54 % of adult drivers have driven a vehicle while feeling drowsy and 28 % of them actually fell asleep on the wheel [6]. Powell et al. [9] concluded that sleepiness can impair driving performance as much or more than alcohol. A more recent report [13] from The American Automobile Association (AAA) estimates that one out of every six (16.5 %) deadly traffic accidents, and one out of eight (12.5 %) crashes requiring hospitalization of car drivers or passengers is due to drowsy driving. In summary, there is a substantial amount of evidence that suggests that drowsiness is one of the big factors in road accidents.

1.2   What Is Drowsiness?

Drowsiness, also referred to as *sleepiness*, can be defined as "the need to fall asleep". This process is a result of normal human biological rhythm, which consists of sleep-wake cycles. The sleep-wake cycle is governed by both homeostatic and circadian factors. Homeostasis relates to the neurobiological need to sleep; the longer the

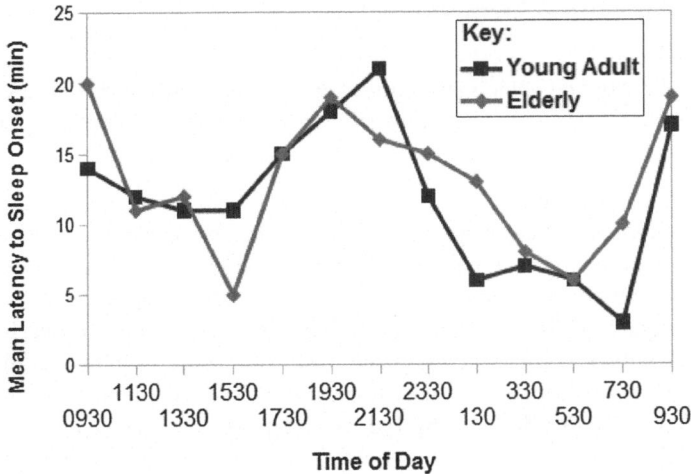

Fig. 1.2 Latency to sleep at 2-h intervals across the 24-h day

period of wakefulness, the more pressure builds for sleep and the more difficult it is to resist [4]. The circadian pacemaker is an internal body clock that completes a cycle approximately every 24 h. Homeostatic factors govern circadian factors to regulate the timing of sleepiness and wakefulness.

These processes create a predictable pattern of two sleepiness peaks, which commonly occur about 12 h after the mid-sleep period (during the afternoon for most people who sleep at night) and before the next consolidated sleep period (most commonly at night, before bedtime) [10] (Fig. 1.2).

It is also worth noticing that the sleep-wake cycle is intrinsic and inevitable, not a pattern to which people voluntarily adhere or can decide to ignore. Despite the tendency of society today to give sleep less priority than other activities, sleepiness and performance impairment are neurobiological responses of the human brain to sleep deprivation.

Sleep and wakefulness are influenced by the light/dark cycle, which in humans most often means wakefulness during daylight and sleep during darkness. People whose sleep is out of phase with this cycle, such as night workers, air crews, and travelers who cross several time zones, can experience sleep loss and sleep disruption that reduce alertness [5, 12].

In medical terms, sleep can be divided into three stages: awake, non-rapid eye movement stage (NREM) and rapid eye movement stage (REM). The sleepy (drowsy) interval—i.e, transition from awake to asleep—occurs during the NREM stage [1].

1.3   What Causes Drowsiness?

Although alcohol and some medications can independently induce sleepiness, the primary causes of sleepiness and drowsy driving in people without sleep disorders are sleep restriction, sleep fragmentation and circadian factors.

Sleep Restriction or Loss
  Short duration of sleep appears to have the greatest negative effects on alertness [11]. Although the need for sleep varies among individuals, sleeping 8 h per 24-h period is common, and 7–9 h is needed to optimize performance. Experimental evidence shows that sleeping less than 4 consolidated hours per night impairs performance on vigilance tasks [8]. Acute sleep loss, even the loss of one night of sleep, results in extreme sleepiness. The effects of sleep loss are cumulative [2]. Regularly losing 1–2 h of sleep a night can create a "sleep debt" and lead to chronic sleepiness over time. The only way to reduce sleep debt is to get some sleep. Both external and internal factors can lead to a restriction in the time available for sleep. External factors include work hours, job and family responsibilities, and school bus or school opening times. Internal or personal factors sometimes are involuntary, such as a medication effect that interrupts sleep. Often, however, reasons for sleep restriction represent a lifestyle choice, such as the decision to sleep less in order to have more time to work, study, socialize, or engage in other activities.

Sleep Fragmentation
  Sleep is an active process, and adequate time in bed does not mean that adequate sleep has been obtained. Sleep disruption and fragmentation cause inadequate sleep and can negatively affect functioning [3]. Similar to sleep restriction, sleep fragmentation can have internal and external causes. The primary internal cause is illness, including untreated sleep disorders. Externally, disturbances such as noise, children, activity and lights, a restless spouse, or job-related duties (e.g., workers who are on call) can interrupt and reduce the quality and quantity of sleep. Studies of commercial vehicle drivers present similar findings. For example, the National Transportation Safety Board (NTSB) [7] concluded that the critical factors in predicting crashes related to sleepiness were: the duration of the most recent sleep period, the amount of sleep in the previous 24 h, and fragmented sleep patterns.

Circadian Factors
  As noted earlier, the circadian pacemaker regularly produces feelings of sleepiness during the afternoon and evening, even among people who are not sleep deprived [3]. Shift work also can disturb sleep by interfering with circadian sleep patterns.

1.4 What Can We Do About It?

In this chapter, we have presented the problem of driver drowsiness and its correlation with car accidents worldwide. The gravity of the problem, and the fact that it is related to a natural physiological need to combat the fatigue of the human system, suggest that it can not be eliminated altogether. Instead, it needs to be measured and detected in time to prevent more serious consequences. In the remainder of this monograph, we will describe several different methods for measuring and detecting driver drowsiness, survey existing solutions, provide guidance on how they can be implemented, and discuss the associated technical challenges.

References

1. V. Brodbeck, A. Kuhn, F. von Wegner, A. Morzelewski, E. Tagliazucchi, S. Borisov, C. M. Michel, and H. Laufs. Eeg microstates of wakefulness and nrem sleep. *NeuroImage*, 62(3):2129–2139, 2012.
2. M. A. Carskadon and W. C. Dement. Cumulative effects of sleep restriction on daytime sleepiness. *Psychophysiology*, 18(2):107–13, 1981.
3. D. Dinges. An overview of sleepiness and accidents. *J Sleep Res*, 4(S2):4–14, 1995.
4. T. Åkertedt, P. Fredlung, M. Gillberg, and B. Jansson. A prospective study of fatal occupational accidents—relationship to sleeping difficulties and occupational factors. *Journal of Sleep Research*, 11(1):69–71, 2002.
5. T. Åkertedt and Torbjorn. Work hours, sleepiness and accidents introduction and summary. *Journal of Sleep Research*, 4:1–3, 1995.
6. R. R. Knipling and J.-S. Wang. Crashes and fatalities related to driver drowsiness/fatigue. Technical report, National Highway Traffic Safety Administration, November 1994.
7. R. A. McMurray. Safety recommendation. Technical report, National Transportation Safety Board, February 2009.
8. P. Naitoh, N. H. R. C. (U.S.), U. S. N. M. Research, and D. Command. *Minimal Sleep to Maintain Performance: Search for Sleep Quantum in Sustained Operations*. Report (Naval Health Research Center). Naval Health Research Center, 1989.
9. Powell N.B. and Schechtman K.B. and Riley R.W. The road to danger: the comparative risks of driving while sleepy. *The Laryngoscope*, 111(5):887–893, May 2001.
10. G. S. Richardson, M. A. Carskadon, E. J. Orav, and W. C. Dement. Circadian variation of sleep tendency in elderly and young adult subjects. *Sleep*, 5 Suppl 2:S82–94, 1982.
11. L. Rosenthal, T. A. Roehrs, A. Rosen, and T. Roth. Level of sleepiness and total sleep time following various time in bed conditions. *Sleep*, 16(3):226–32, 1993.
12. A. Samel, H. M. Wegmann, and M. Vejvoda. Jet lag and sleepiness In aircrew. *Journal of Sleep Research*, 4(s2):30–36, 1995.
13. B. C. Tefft. Asleep at the wheel: the prevalence and impact of drowsy driving. Technical report, American Automobile Association Foundation for Traffic Safety, November 2010.
14. World Health Organization. *Global status report on road safety: summary*. World Health Organization, 2009.
15. World Health Organization. *Global Status Report on Road Safety 2013: Supporting a Decade of Action : Summary*. World Health Organization, 2013.

Chapter 2
Driver Drowsiness Detection and Measurement Methods

There are several different ways to detect and measure driver drowsiness (or sleepiness). They are normally grouped into five categories: subjective, physiological, vehicle-based, behavioral, and hybrid. This chapter provides a brief survey of driver drowsiness detection methods in each of these categories.

2.1 Subjective Methods

Sleepiness can be explained as a physiological need to combat the fatigue of the human system. The more the system is fatigued (i.e., sleep deprived), the stronger the need for sleep, which suggests that sleepiness can have different levels. Scientific organizations such as *Laboratory for Sleep* [45], *Division of Sleep Disorders* [45] and *Association of Professional Sleep Societies* [7], to name a few, have been creating various descriptive scales of sleepiness levels.

Current subjective tools used for the assessment of sleepiness are based on questionnaires and electro-physiological measures of sleep. Their purpose is to provide an insight on how to more successfully predict which factors might lead to accidents and to provide means for other method groups to focus on detecting and preventing some key factors associated with driver drowsiness.

This way of measuring is known as *Subjective Measuring*, since testing subjects were asked to describe their level of sleepiness, which is clearly a subjective assessment of their perception of drowsiness.

Some of the best-known subjective tests of sleepiness are:

- **Epworth Sleepiness Scale (ESS)** [27]: an eight-item, self-report measure that quantifies individuals' sleepiness by their tendency to fall asleep in static, non-stressful situations: reading, watching television, sitting in a car at a traffic light. On each of eight situations, subjects are rating their likeliness to doze off or

© The Author(s) 2014
A. Čolić et al., *Driver Drowsiness Detection*, SpringerBriefs in Computer Science,
DOI 10.1007/978-3-319-11535-1__2

Table 2.1 Typical administration of MSLT test

Step	Time	Subject's Chores
1	5 AM	Lights on
2	7 AM	Subject awake
3	7:30 AM	Measuring brain activity
4	8 AM	20 min nap
5	9 AM	Subject awake—measuring brain activity
6	10 AM	20 min nap
7	12:30 PM	Subject eats lunch—measuring brain activity
8	1 PM	20 min nap
9	3:30 PM	Subject leaves

fall asleep on a scale from 0 (no chance) to 3 (high chance). Subjects can score between 0 and 24 points. Subjects scoring less than 10 are considered awake or slightly sleepy, while 15 points or more indicate severe sleepiness.

- **Multiple Sleep Latency Test (MSLT)** [7]: a test based on the presumption that people who fall asleep faster are more sleep deprived. The MSLT measures the tendency to fall asleep in a standardized sleep-promoting situation during four or five 20-min nap opportunities that are spaced 2 h apart throughout the day and in which the individual is instructed to try to fall asleep (Table 2.1). Since brain wave sleep-staging criteria are very well established, the intervals of time it takes the subjects to fall asleep can be easily measured. If a subject needs less than 5 min to fall asleep, he or she is considered pathologically sleepy; whereas taking more then 10 min is considered normal.
- **Maintenance of Wakefulness Test (MWT)** [45]: a test in which individuals are instructed to try and remain awake. Their attempt is monitored over a period of 20 min. If a subject can stay awake over that period of time, he is considered awake and capable of operating a vehicle. But if a subject falls asleep within the first 15 min, he can be considered too sleep deprived to drive.
- **Stanford Sleepiness Scale (SSS)** [21]: an instrument that contains seven statements through which people rate their current level of alertness (e.g., 1= "feeling...wide awake" to 7= "...sleep onset soon..."). The scale correlates with standard performance measures, is sensitive to sleep loss and can be administered repeatedly throughout a 24-h period. Typically, subjects are asked to rate their alertness level every 2 h throughout the day by choosing a single number associated with specific alertness description (Table 2.2).
- **The Karolinska Sleepiness Scale (KSS)** [2]: contains questions that guide subjects to provide, to the best of their ability, a self-report of the quality of their sleep. Laboratory tests and field studies suggest that the measurements gathered by this method seem to adequately cover and relate to various sleep and lack of sleep scenarios. This is the most commonly used drowsiness scale—a nine-point scale that has verbal anchors for each step (Table 2.3).

Table 2.2 Stanford Sleepiness Scale

Value	Description
1	Feeling active, vital, alert or wide awake
2	Functioning at high levels, but not at peak; able to concentrate
3	Relaxed, awake but not fully alert; responsive
4	Little foggy
5	Foggy, beginning to loose track; having difficulty staying awake
6	Sleepy, woozy, fighting sleep; prefer to lie down
7	Cannot stay awake, sleep onset appears imminent

Table 2.3 Karolinska Sleepiness Scale verbal cues

Level	Sleepiness level
1	Extremely alert
2	Very alert
3	Alert
4	Rather alert
5	Neither alert nor sleepy
6	Some signs of sleepiness
7	Sleepy but no difficulty staying awake
8	Sleepy with some effort to keep alert
9	Extremely sleepy, fighting sleep

- **Visual Analogue Scale (VAS)** [65]: asks subjects to rate their "sleepiness" using a scale spread along a 100 mm wide line. Suggestions for sleep deprivation state range from "just about asleep" (left end) to "as wide awake as I can be" (right end). Subjects place a mark on the line expressing how sleepy they feel they are. Sleepiness level is measured by the distance in millimeters from one end of the scale to the mark placed on the line. The VAS is convenient since it can be rapidly administered as well as easily repeated.

The MSLT and MWT were developed for neurophysiological assessment and are sensitive to both acute and chronic sleep loss. These types of tests cannot be administered and monitored without special training and under special conditions and can only be performed on healthy subjects [7, 45]. Moreover, the practicality of these tests for assessing crashes is very small but some portions of them, such as slightly modified "nap tests" in combination with questionnaires, have been used for that purpose [51].

Other subjective measurement methods worth mentioning are: Sleep-Wake Activity Inventory [54], Pittsburgh Sleep Quality Index [6] and Sleep Disorders Questionnaire [14]. All of them are not quite practical for assessment of crash situations but their ability to monitor individuals over extended periods of time, combined with subjects' self-reporting provides valuable information towards better understanding of sleep deprivation and its manifestation in humans.

Subjective measurement results gathered from all these tests greatly depend on the quality of the asked questions as well as proper interpretation and understanding of those questions by the subject. Due to the age and social diversity of subjects, it might not be possible to formulate a questionnaire to accommodate every potential problem. Moreover, the subjects' perspective plays a huge role on the quality of the acquired data. Lastly, it is worth stating that it is very difficult to acquire subjective drowsiness feedback from a driver in a real-world driving situation; all the measurements are usually done in a simulated environment.

2.2 Physiological Methods

Physiological methods offer an objective, precise way to measure sleepiness. They are based upon the fact that physiological signals start to change in earlier stages of drowsiness [3, 30], which could allow a potential driver drowsiness detection system a little bit of extra time to alert a drowsy driver in a timely manner and thereby prevent many road accidents. The idea of being able to detect drowsiness at an early stage with very few false positives has motivated many researchers to experiment with various electro-physiological signals of the human body, such as electrocardiogram (ECG), electroencephalogram (EEG), and electrooculogram (EOG). They are briefly defined and explained below.

- **Electrocardiogram (ECG)** records electrical activity of a human heart. This system can very precisely tell which state the human body is in by detecting minute changes in the behavior of the heart, such as increase or decrease of heart rate [28, 50]. Variability of a heart rate can be described using Heart Rate Variability measure (HRV) [28, 50], in which the low (LF) and high (HF) frequencies of heartbeat are described. HRV is a measure of the beat-to-beat (R-R intervals) changes in the heart rate. When a subject is awake, the heart rate is much closer to the HF. The ECG can clearly show that when a subject starts going into drowsy state, the heart rate starts slowing down and heading towards the LF band.
- **Electroencephalogram (EEG)** records electrical activity of a human brain. It is the most reliable and most commonly used signal that can precisely describe humans alertness level [3, 27, 36, 37, 40]. The EEG signal is highly complex and has various frequency bands. Frequency bands that can be measured to determine if a subject is drowsy are: delta band—which corresponds to sleep activity; theta band—which is related to drowsiness; and beta band—which corresponds to alertness. A decrease in the power changes in the alpha frequency band and an increase in the theta frequency band indicate drowsiness. The frequencies measured using this method are very prone to errors and require very specific conditions for being measured properly. Moreover, in order to measure them, sensing devices would have to make physical contact with the subject. Clearly, in

a real-world driving scenario, having electrodes attached to the driver's head, beyond their huge inconvenience, would hinder their driving capabilities and potentially increase the chances of an accident happening.

- **Electrooculogram (EOG)** records the electrical potential difference between the cornea and the retina of a human eye. It is shown that this difference determines the behavior of the eye, which can be used to monitor drivers' alertness level [24, 28, 31]. This method is highly invasive since it requires direct contact with a subject, usually in the following manner: a disposable electrode is placed on the outer corner of each eye and a third electrode at the center of the forehead for reference [34]. The associated methodology is relatively simple: if a slower eye movement is detected, compared to the regular eye movement of a subject in the awake stage, the conclusion is that the subject is becoming drowsy. Though this type of measurement is very precise and leads to very small detection errors, it is not the most practical for real-world, real-time implementation due to its invasiveness and the complexity of the apparatus needed for the measurement.

The reliability and accuracy of driver drowsiness detection by using physiological signals is very high compared to other methods. However, the intrusive nature of measuring physiological signals remains an issue that prevents their use in real-world scenarios. Due to the technological progress in recent years, it is possible that some of the problems caused by these methods will be overcome in the future. Examples include: the use of wireless devices to measure physiological signals in a less intrusive manner by placing the electrodes on the body and obtaining signals using wireless technologies like Zigbee or Bluetooth; or by placing electrodes on the steering wheel [17, 68]; or placing electrodes on the drivers seat [4]. The obtained signals can be processed and monitored in various ways, such as using smart phone devices [20, 32]. Obtaining these signals in a non-intrusive way certainly contributes towards their real-world applicability. But the question on whether this way of collecting data may lead to increased measurement errors has not been answered conclusively yet. Recently, a few experiments have been conducted to validate the potential use of less-intrusive or non-intrusive systems and inspect the implications of this trade-off [4, 17].

2.3   Vehicle-Based Methods

Our understanding of drowsy-driving crashes is often based on subjective evidence, such as police crash reports and driver's self-reports following the event [43, 49]. Evidence gathered from the reports suggests that the typical drivers' and vehicles' behavior during these events usually exhibit characteristics such as:

- **Higher speed with little or no breaking**. Fall-asleep crashes are likely to have serious consequences. The mortality rate associated with drowsy-driving crashes is high, probably due to the combination of higher speeds and delayed reaction time [23].

- **A vehicle leaves the roadway**. An analysis of police crash reports in North Carolina showed that the majority of the non alcohol, drowsy-driving crashes were single-vehicle roadway departures [49]. It is very common for a sleep-impaired driver to lose concentration and stray off the road. The NHTSA General Estimates System data reflects the same trend but also suggests that sleepiness may play a role in rear-end crashes and head-on crashes as well [29].
- **The crash occurs on a high-speed road**. In comparison with other types of crashes, drowsy-driving crashes more often take place on highways and major roadways with speed limits of 55 miles per hour and higher [29]. It seems that monotonous driving on such roads can cause lapses in concentration on sleep deprived drivers thus increasing a chance of an accident.
- **The driver does not attempt to avoid crashing**. NHTSA data shows that sleepy drivers are less likely than alert drivers to take corrective action before a crash [29]. Reports also suggest that evidence of a corrective maneuver, such as skid marks or brake lights, is usually absent in a fall-asleep crash.
- **The driver is alone in the vehicle**. In a New York State survey of lifetime incidents, 82 % of drowsy-driving crashes involved a single occupant [43].

All of the characteristics noted above suggest that a vehicle involved in an accident driven by a drowsy driver creates specific driving patterns that can be measured and used for detection of a potential drowsy driving situation.

The two most commonly used vehicle-based measures for driver drowsiness detection are: the steering wheel movement (SWM) and the standard deviation of lane position (SDLP).

Steering Wheel Movement (SWM) These methods rely on measuring the steering wheel angle using an angle sensor mounted on the steering column, which allows for detection of even the slightest steering wheel position changes [15, 48, 57]. When the driver is drowsy, the number of micro-corrections on the steering wheel is lower than the one found in normal driving conditions [15, 16]. A potential problem with this approach is the high number of false positives. SWM-based systems can function reliably only in particular environments and are too dependent on the geometric characteristics of the road and, to a lesser extent, on the kinetic characteristics of the vehicle [62].

Standard Deviation of Lane Position (SDLP) Leaving a designated lane and crossing into a lane of opposing traffic or going off the road are typical behaviors of a car driven by a driver who has fallen asleep. The core idea behind SDLP is to monitor the car's relative position within its lane with an externally-mounted camera. Specialized software is used to analyze the data acquired by the camera and compute the car's position relative to the road's middle lane [25, 61]. SDLP-based systems' limitations are mostly tied to their dependence on external factors such as: road marking, weather, and lighting conditions.

2.4   Behavioral Methods

The methods mentioned thus far were deemed as either unreliable or very intrusive for real-world applications, thus leading towards exploiting a different type of methodology, based upon non-invasive observation of a driver's external state. These methods are based on detecting specific behavioral clues exhibited by a driver while in a drowsy state. A typical focus is on facial expressions that might express characteristics such as: rapid, constant blinking, nodding or swinging of the head, or frequent yawning. These are all tell-tale signs that a person might be sleep deprived and/or feeling drowsy. Typically, systems based on this methodology use a video camera for image acquisition and rely on a combination of computer vision and machine learning techniques to detect events of interest, measure them, and make a decision on whether the driver may be drowsy or not. If the sequence of captured images and measured parameters (e.g., pattern of nodding or time lapsed in "closed eye state") suggest that the driver is drowsy, an action—such as sounding an audible alarm—might be warranted.

- **Head or eye position**. When a driver is drowsy, some of the muscles in the body begin to relax, leading to nodding. This nodding behavior is what researchers are trying to detect. Research exploiting this feature has started just recently [47, 69]. Detecting head or eye position is a complex computer vision problem which might require stereoscopic vision or 3D vision cameras.
- **Yawning**. Frequent yawning is a behavioral feature that tells that the body is fatigued or falling into a more relaxed state, leading towards sleepiness. Detecting yawning can serve as a preemptive measure to alert the driver. It should be noted, however, that yawning does not always occur before the driver goes into a drowsy state. Therefore it cannot be used as a stand-alone feature; it needs to be backed up with additional indicators of sleepiness. Examples of research in this area include the work of Smith, Shah, and da Vitoria Lobo [56], and more recently by Saradadevi et al. [55].
- **Eye state**. Detecting the state of the eyes has been the main focus of research for determining if a driver is drowsy or not. In particular, the frequency of blinking has been observed [1, 5, 11, 13, 39, 44]. The term PERCLOS (PERcentage of eyelid CLOSure over the pupil over time) has been devised to provide a meaningful way to correlate drowsiness with frequency of blinking. This measurement has been found to be a reliable measure to predict drowsiness.

    At any given time, the eye can roughly be categorized into one of three states: wide open, partially open, or closed. The last two can be used as indicators that a driver is experiencing sleepiness. If the eyes stay in these two states for a prolonged period of time, it can be concluded that the driver is experiencing abnormal behavior. An eye-state detection system must be able to reliably detect and distinguish these different states of the eyes. Various algorithms with various approaches for extracting and filtering important features of the eyes [33, 35, 52, 53, 64] have been used throughout the years. Typically, the feature extraction process is followed by training and use of machine learning algorithms of various capabilities, strengths and weaknesses [9, 12, 18, 19, 22, 26, 38, 41, 42, 58–60, 63, 66].

- **Multiple Facial Actions**. Some researchers used multiple facial features, including state and position of the eyebrow, lip and jaw dropping combined with eye blinking [10].

Behavioral methods are considered cost effective and non-invasive, but lead to significant technical challenges. In addition to the challenges associated with the underlying computer vision, machine learning and image processing algorithms, the resulting systems are required to perform in real-time and to exhibit robustness when faced with bumpy roads, lighting changes, dirty lenses, improperly mounted cameras, and many other real-world less-than-ideal driving situations.

2.5 Hybrid Methods

All of the previously mentioned methods have strengths and weaknesses. Vehicle-based measurements depend on specific driving conditions (such as weather, lighting, etc.) and can be used on specific roads only (with clearly marked signs and lanes). Moreover, they may lead to a large number of false positives, which would lead to a loss of confidence in the method. Behavioral measures, on the other hand, may show huge variation in the results depending on the associated lighting conditions. Physiological measures are reliable and accurate but their intrusive nature is still a challenge, which may be mitigated should non-invasive physiological sensors become feasible in the near future [32, 46].

Several recent research studies have attempted to develop driver drowsiness detection systems as a fusion of different methods. One study which combined behavioral methodology and vehicle-based methodology showed that the reliability and accuracy of the created hybrid method was significantly higher than those using a single methodology approach [8]. Another study, which included subjective measures in combination with behavioral and physiological measures, showed significantly higher success rate than any individual method alone [67]. These early results suggest that a combination of the three types of methods—behavioral, physiological and vehicle-based—is a promising avenue worth pursuing in the development of real-world, vehicle-mounted, driver drowsiness detection solutions.

References

1. T. Abe, T. Nonomura, Y. Komada, S. Asaoka, T. Sasai, A. Ueno, and Y. Inoue. Detecting deteriorated vigilance using percentage of eyelid closure time during behavioral maintenance of wakefulness tests. *International Journal of Psychophysiology*, 82(3):269–274, 2011.

2. T. Akerstedt, K. Hume, D. Minors, and J. Waterhouse. The subjective meaning of good sleep, an intraindividual approach using the Karolinska sleep diary. *Percept Mot Skills*, 79(1 Pt 1):287–96, 1994.

3. M. Akin, M. B. Kurt, N. Sezgin, and M. Bayram. Estimating vigilance level by using EEG and EMG signals. *Neural Comput. Appl.*, 17(3):227–236, Apr. 2008.

4. H. J. Baek, G. S. Chung, K. K. Kim, and K.-S. Park. A smart health monitoring chair for nonintrusive measurement of biological signals. *Information Technology in Biomedicine, IEEE Transactions on*, 16(1):150–158, 2012.

5. L. Bergasa, J. Nuevo, M. Sotelo, R. Barea, and M. Lopez. Real-time system for monitoring driver vigilance. *Intelligent Transportation Systems, IEEE Transactions on*, 7(1):63–77, 2006.

6. D. J. Buysse, C. F. Reynolds III, T. H. Monk, S. R. Berman, and D. J. Kupfer. The Pittsburgh sleep quality index: A new instrument for psychiatric practice and research. *Psychiatry Research*, 28:193–213, 1989.

7. Carskadon MA and Dement WC and Mitler MM and Roth T and Westbrook PR and Keenan S. Guidelines for the multiple sleep latency test (MSLT): a standard measure of sleepiness. *Sleep*, 9:519–524, 1989.

8. B. Cheng, W. Zhang, Y. Lin, R. Feng, and X. Zhang. Driver drowsiness detection based on multisource information. *Human Factors and Ergonomics in Manufacturing and Service Industries*, 22(5):450–467, 2012.

9. E. Cheng, B. Kong, R. Hu, and F. Zheng. Eye state detection in facial image based on linear prediction error of wavelet coefficients. In *Robotics and Biomimetics, 2008. ROBIO 2008. IEEE International Conference on*, pages 1388–1392, 2009.

10. M. Dehnavi, N. Attarzadeh, and M. Eshghi. Real time eye state recognition. In *Electrical Engineering (ICEE), 2011 19th Iranian Conference on*, pages 1–4, 2011.

11. D. Dinges and U. S. N. H. T. S. Administration. *Evaluation of Techniques for Ocular Measurement as an Index of Fatigue and as the Basis for Alertness Management*. United States. Dept. of Transportation. National Highway Traffic Safety Administration, 1998.

12. W. Dong and P. Qu. Eye state classification based on multi-feature fusion. In *Control and Decision Conference, 2009. CCDC '09. Chinese*, pages 231–234, 2009.

13. T. D'Orazio, M. Leo, C. Guaragnella, and A. Distante. A visual approach for driver inattention detection. *Pattern Recognition*, 40(8):2341–2355, 2007.

14. A. B. Douglass, R. Bornstein, G. Nino-Murcia, S. Keenan, L. Miles, V. P. Zarcone, C. Guilleminault, and W. C. Dement. The sleep disorders questionnaire. i: Creation and multivariate structure of SDQ. *Sleep*, 17(2):160–7, 1994.

15. S. H. Fairclough and R. Graham. Impairment of driving performance caused by sleep deprivation or alcohol: A comparative study. *Human Factors: The Journal of the Human Factors and Ergonomics Society*, 41(1):118–128, 1999.

16. R. Feng, G. Zhang, and B. Cheng. An on-board system for detecting driver drowsiness based on multi-sensor data fusion using Dempster-Shafer theory. In *Networking, Sensing and Control, 2009. ICNSC '09. International Conference on Networking*, pages 897–902, 2009.

17. J. Gomez-Clapers and R. Casanella. A fast and easy-to-use ECG acquisition and heart rate monitoring system using a wireless steering wheel. *Sensors Journal, IEEE*, 12(3):610–616, 2012.

18. J. Guo and X. Guo. Eye state recognition based on shape analysis and fuzzy logic. In *Intelligent Vehicles Symposium, 2009 IEEE*, pages 78–82, 2009.

19. R. Hammoud, A. Wilhelm, P. Malawey, and G. Witt. Efficient real-time algorithms for eye state and head pose tracking in advanced driver support systems. In *Computer Vision and Pattern Recognition, 2005. CVPR 2005. IEEE Computer Society Conference on*, volume 2, pages 1181 vol. 2–, 2005.

20. P.-C. Hii and W.-Y. Chung. A comprehensive ubiquitous healthcare solution on an Android™ mobile device. *Sensors*, 11(7):6799–6815, 2011.

21. E. Hoddes, V. Zarcone, H. Smythe, R. Phillips, and W. C. Dement. Quantification of sleepiness: a new approach. *Psychophysiology*, 10(4):431–6, 1973.

22. T. Hong, H. Qin, and Q. Sun. An improved real time eye state identification system in driver drowsiness detection. In *Control and Automation, 2007. ICCA 2007. IEEE International Conference on*, pages 1449–1453, 2007.

23. J. A. Horne and L. A. Reyner. Sleep related vehicle accidents. *BMJ*, 310(6979):565–567, 3 1995.

24. S. Hu and G. Zheng. Driver drowsiness detection with eyelid related parameters by Support Vector Machine. *Expert Syst. Appl.*, 36(4):7651–7658, May 2009.

25. M. Ingre, T. Akerstedt, B. Peters, A. Anund, and G. Kecklund. Subjective sleepiness, simulated driving performance and blink duration: examining individual differences. *Journal of Sleep Research*, 15(1):47–53, 2006.

26. C. Jiangwei, J. Lisheng, G. Lie, G. Keyou, and W. Rongben. Driver's eye state detecting method design based on eye geometry feature. In *Intelligent Vehicles Symposium, 2004 IEEE*, pages 357–362, 2004.

27. M. Johns. A new method for measuring daytime sleepiness: the Epworth sleepiness scale. *Sleep*, 14(6):540–5, 1991.

28. R. Khushaba, S. Kodagoda, S. Lal, and G. Dissanayake. Driver drowsiness classification using fuzzy wavelet-packet-based feature-extraction algorithm. *Biomedical Engineering, IEEE Transactions on*, 58(1):121–131, 2011.

29. R. Knipling, J. Wang, and M. J. Goodman. The role of driver inattention in crashes: New statistics from the 1995 crashworthiness data system. *Annual proceedings of the Association for the Advancement of Automotive Medicine*, 40:377–392, 1996.

30. A. Kokonozi, E. Michail, I. C. Chouvarda, and N. Maglaveras. A study of heart rate and brain system complexity and their interaction in sleep-deprived subjects. In *Computers in Cardiology, 2008*, pages 969–971, 2008.

31. M. B. Kurt, N. Sezgin, M. Akin, G. Kirbas, and M. Bayram. The ANN-based computing of drowsy level. *Expert Systems with Applications*, 36(2, Part 1):2534–2542, 2009.

32. B.-G. Lee and W.-Y. Chung. Multi-classifier for highly reliable driver drowsiness detection in Android platform. *Biomedical Engineering: Applications, Basis and Communications*, 24(02):147–154, 2012.

33. A. Lenskiy and J.-S. Lee. Driver's eye blinking detection using novel color and texture segmentation algorithms. *International Journal of Control, Automation and Systems*, 10(2):317–327, 2012.

34. W. C. Liang, J. Yuan, D. C. Sun, and M. H. Lin. Changes in physiological parameters induced by indoor simulated driving: Effect of lower body exercise at mid-term break. *Sensors*, 9(9):6913–6933, 2009.

35. C.-C. Lien and P.-R. Lin. Drowsiness recognition using the Least Correlated LBPH. In *Intelligent Information Hiding and Multimedia Signal Processing (IIH-MSP), 2012 Eighth International Conference on*, pages 158–161, 2012.

36. C.-T. Lin, C.-J. Chang, B.-S. Lin, S.-H. Hung, C.-F. Chao, and I.-J. Wang. A real-time wireless brain - computer interface system for drowsiness detection. *Biomedical Circuits and Systems, IEEE Transactions on*, 4(4):214–222, 2010.

37. F.-C. Lin, L.-W. Ko, C.-H. Chuang, T.-P. Su, and C.-T. Lin. Generalized EEG-based drowsiness prediction system by using a self-organizing neural fuzzy system. *IEEE Trans. on Circuits and Systems*, 59-I(9):2044–2055, 2012.

38. A. Liu, Z. Li, L. Wang, and Y. Zhao. A practical driver fatigue detection algorithm based on eye state. In *Microelectronics and Electronics (PrimeAsia), 2010 Asia Pacific Conference on Postgraduate Research in*, pages 235–238, 2010.

39. D. Liu, P. Sun, Y. Xiao, and Y. Yin. Drowsiness detection based on eyelid movement. In *Education Technology and Computer Science (ETCS), 2010 Second International Workshop on*, volume 2, pages 49–52, 2010.

40. J. Liu, C. Zhang, and C. Zheng. EEG-based estimation of mental fatigue by using KPCA–HMM and complexity parameters. *Biomedical Signal Processing and Control*, 5(2):124–130, 2010.

41. W. Liu, Y. Wang, and L. Jia. An effective eye states detection method based on projection. In *Signal Processing (ICSP), 2010 IEEE 10th International Conference on*, pages 829–831, 2010.

42. Z. Liu and H. Ai. Automatic eye state recognition and closed-eye photo correction. In *Pattern Recognition, 2008. ICPR 2008. 19th International Conference on*, pages 1–4, 2008.

43. A. T. McCartt, S. A. Ribner, A. I. Pack, and M. C. Hammer. The scope and nature of the drowsy driving problem in New York State. *Accident Analysis and Prevention*, 28(4):511–517, 1996.

44. R. A. McKinley, L. K. McIntire, R. Schmidt, D. W. Repperger, and J. A. Caldwell. Evaluation of eye metrics as a detector of fatigue. *Human Factors: The Journal of the Human Factors and Ergonomics Society*, 53(4):403–414, 2011.

45. M. M. Mitler, K. S. Gujavarty, and C. P. Browman. Maintenance of wakefulness test: a polysomnographic technique for evaluation treatment efficacy in patients with excessive somnolence. *Electroencephalogr Clin Neurophysiol*, 53(6):658–61, 1982.

46. A. Mizuno, H. Okumura, and M. Matsumura. Development of neckband mounted active bio-electrodes for non-restraint lead method of ECG R wave. In J. Sloten, P. Verdonck, M. Nyssen, and J. Haueisen, editors, *4th European Conference of the International Federation for Medical and Biological Engineering*, volume 22 of *IFMBE Proceedings*, pages 1394–1397. Springer Berlin Heidelberg, 2009.

47. E. Murphy-Chutorian and M. Trivedi. Head pose estimation and augmented reality tracking: An integrated system and evaluation for monitoring driver awareness. *Intelligent Transportation Systems, IEEE Transactions on*, 11(2):300–311, 2010.

48. S. Otmani, T. Pebayle, J. Roge, and A. Muzet. Effect of driving duration and partial sleep deprivation on subsequent alertness and performance of car drivers. *Physiology and Behavior*, 84(5):715–724, 2005.

49. A. I. Pack, A. M. Pack, E. Rodgman, A. Cucchiara, D. F. Dinges, and C. Schwab. Characteristics of crashes attributed to the driver having fallen asleep. *Accident Analysis and Prevention*, 27(6):769–775, 1995.

50. M. Patel, S. K. L. Lal, D. Kavanagh, and P. Rossiter. Applying neural network analysis on heart rate variability data to assess driver fatigue. *Expert Syst. Appl.*, 38(6):7235–7242, June 2011.

51. P. Philip, I. Ghorayeb, D. Leger, J. Menny, B. Bioulac, P. Dabadie, and C. Guilleminault. Objective measurement of sleepiness in summer vacation long-distance drivers. *Electroencephalogr Clin Neurophysiol*, 102(5):383–9, 1997.

52. H. Qin, J. Liu, and T. Hong. An eye state identification method based on the Embedded Hidden Markov Model. In *Vehicular Electronics and Safety (ICVES), 2012 IEEE International Conference on*, pages 255–260, 2012.

53. C. Qingzhang, W. Wenfu, and C. Yuqin. Research on eye-state based monitoring for drivers' dozing. *Intelligent Information Technology Applications, 2007 Workshop on*, 1:373–376, 2009.

54. L. Rosenthal, T. A. Roehrs, and T. Roth. The sleep-wake activity inventory: A self-report measure of daytime sleepiness. *Biological Psychiatry*, 34(11):810–820, 1993.

55. M. Saradadevi and P. Bajaj. Driver fatigue detection using Mouth and Yawning analysis. *International Journal of Computer Science and Network Security*, 8(6):183–188, 2008.

56. P. Smith, M. Shah, and N. da Vitoria Lobo. Determining driver visual attention with one camera. *Intelligent Transportation Systems, IEEE Transactions on*, 4(4):205–218, 2003.

57. P. Thiffault and J. Bergeron. Monotony of road environment and driver fatigue: a simulator study. *Accident Analysis and Prevention*, 35(3):381–391, 2003.

58. Y.-l. Tian, T. Kanade, and J. F. Cohn. Eye-state action unit detection by Gabor Wavelets. In *Proceedings of the Third International Conference on Advances in Multimodal Interfaces*, ICMI '00, pages 143–150, London, UK, UK, 2000. Springer-Verlag.

59. Z. Tian and H. Qin. Real-time driver's eye state detection. In *Vehicular Electronics and Safety, 2005. IEEE International Conference on*, pages 285–289, 2005.

60. N. H. Villaroman and D. C. Rowe. Improving accuracy in face tracking user interfaces using consumer devices. In *Proceedings of the 1st Annual conference on Research in information technology*, RIIT '12, pages 57–62, New York, NY, USA, 2012. ACM.

61. Volvo. Volvo driver alert control and lane departure warning system. http://www.zercustoms. com/news/Volvo-Driver-Alert-Control-and-Lane-Departure-Warning.html, 2007.

62. E. Vural. *Video Based Detection of Driver Fatigue*. PhD thesis, Sabanci University, 2009.

63. F. Wang, M. Zhou, and B. Zhu. A novel feature based rapid eye state detection method. In *Robotics and Biomimetics (ROBIO), 2009 IEEE International Conference on*, pages 1236–1240, 2009.

64. H. Wang, L. Zhou, and Y. Ying. A novel approach for real time eye state detection in fatigue awareness system. In *Robotics Automation and Mechatronics (RAM), 2010 IEEE Conference on*, pages 528–532, 2010.

65. M. E. Wewers and N. K. Lowe. A critical review of visual analogue scales in the measurement of clinical phenomena. *Res Nurs Health*, 13(4):227–36, 1990.

66. Y.-S. Wu, T.-W. Lee, Q.-Z. Wu, and H.-S. Liu. An eye state recognition method for drowsiness detection. In *Vehicular Technology Conference (VTC 2010-Spring), 2010 IEEE 71st*, pages 1–5, 2010.

67. G. Yang, Y. Lin, and P. Bhattacharya. A driver fatigue recognition model based on information fusion and dynamic bayesian network. *Information Sciences*, 180(10):1942–1954, 2010. <ce:title>Special Issue on Intelligent Distributed Information Systems</ce:title>.

68. X. Yu, U. of Minnesota. Intelligent Transportation Systems Institute, D. D. o. M. University of Minnesota, and I. Engineering. *Real-time Nonintrusive Detection of Driver Drowsiness: Final Report*. CTS (Series : Minneapolis, Minn.). Intelligent Transportation Systems Institute, Center for Transportation Studies, University of Minnesota, 2009.

69. X. Zhang, N. Zheng, F. Mu, and Y. He. Head pose estimation using isophote features for driver assistance systems. In *Intelligent Vehicles Symposium, 2009 IEEE*, pages 568–572, 2009.

Chapter 3
Commercial Solutions

The automobile industry has spent a significant amount of resources in recent years to develop new features aimed at driver drowsiness detection. Moreover, independent companies have also recognized that this market might grow and become profitable and have developed products whose goals are comparable, but work independently of the vehicle's brand or model. This chapter provides a representative sample of those efforts.

3.1 Car Manufacturers

The ability to offer some type of 'driver assist' system as an added value to their vehicle lineup has motivated many automobile manufacturers to offer built-in solutions that are capable of detecting signs of driver drowsiness and warning the driver accordingly. These are some examples (sorted alphabetically by car manufacturer).

- **Ford:** The American car manufacturer introduced their "Driver Alert System" in 2012 [3]. The system uses a forward-looking camera to monitor the vehicle's position in the lane and estimate the driver's alertness level based upon driver behavior, i.e, the ability to stay within the lane's limits. If the alertness level is perceived to be lower than a certain threshold, a light audible and visual warning—"Rest suggested"—appears in the car's instrument cluster; if it falls even further, a more severe alert—"Rest now"—(with red light and chime sound) is displayed until it is explicitly dismissed by the driver. The system also offers

© The Author(s) 2014
A. Čolić et al., *Driver Drowsiness Detection*, SpringerBriefs in Computer Science,
DOI 10.1007/978-3-319-11535-1_3

Fig. 3.1 The Lexus driver
monitoring system uses six
IR sensors (visible
immediately in front of the
instrument panel). Source:
Wikimedia Commons

the possibility to check for the current estimated level of alertness at any given time. This system falls under the "vehicle-based" category[1] of driver drowsiness detection methods.

- **Lexus and Toyota:** The Japanese automaker (part of the Toyota group) has offered, in selected vehicles, a "Driver Monitoring System", which first became available in 2006 [8]. It uses a CCD (charge-coupled device) camera, mounted on top of the steering column cover to monitor driver attentiveness using eye tracking and head motion detection techniques. Six built-in near-infrared LED sensors enable the system to work accurately both day and night (Fig. 3.1). During start up, the system automatically estimates the position of the driver's facial features and measures the width and center line of the face. This information is used as a reference to monitor the movement of the driver's head when looking from side to side (Fig. 3.2).

  The solution works in conjunction with Lexus' "Advanced Obstacle Detection System" as follows. If the driver turns his head away from the road ahead while the vehicle is moving and an obstacle is detected in front of the vehicle, the system activates a pre-crash warning light and buzzer. If the situation persists, the brakes are briefly applied to alert the driver. And if this still fails to elicit action from the driver, the system engages emergency braking preparation and front seatbelt pre-tensioning.

  The combination of different monitoring devices places this system in the "hybrid" category (according to the different categories listed in Chap. 2).

  The "Driver Monitoring System" has been modified in 2008 by Toyota company to include eyelid detection which is used to determine the state of driver's eyes [9]. This increases the overall robustness of the system. If the eyelids

---

[1]Please refer to Chap. 2 for a description of all categories.

Fig. 3.2 Lexus driver
monitoring system. Source:
Wikimedia Commons

DRIVER MONITORING SYSTEM

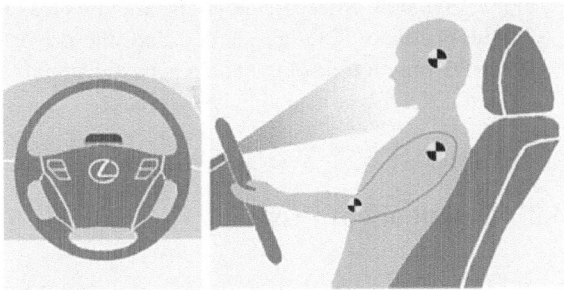

Lexus facial recognition safety system using
infrared sensors to monitor driver alertness

start to get droopy, an alarm will sound, and, again, the system will jump in and
attempt to decelerate the car automatically. Toyota expects to be installing this in
cars in the next couple of years.

- **Mercedes-Benz**. Back in 2009, Mercedes-Benz introduced system called
  "Attention Assist" [4]. At the heart of this system is a highly sensitive sensor
  which allows extremely precise monitoring of the steering wheel movements
  and the steering speed. Based on these data, the system calculates an individual
  behavioral pattern during the first few minutes of every trip. This pattern is
  then continuously compared with the current steering behavior and the current
  driving situation. This process allows the system to detect typical indicators
  of drowsiness and warn the driver. The system becomes active at the speeds
  between 80 and 180 km/h because it has been shown that, while driving for
  extended period of time at these speeds, the risk of drowsiness is much greater
  then in typical city drive.
- **Volvo**. Volvo was among the first to introduce a drowsiness detection system
  [11], combining two safety features: "Driver Alert Control" and "Lane Departure
  Warning". "Driver Alert Control" monitors the car's movements and assesses
  whether the vehicle is being driven in a controlled or uncontrolled way. From
  the technical point of view the system is straight forward and consists of: (a) a
  camera, which is installed between the windshield and the interior rear-view
  mirror and continuously measures the distance between the car and the road
  lane markings; (b) sensors, which register the car's movements; (c) a control
  unit, which stores the information and calculates whether the driver risks losing
  control of the vehicle. The second system, "Lane Departure Warning System",
  helps preventing single-vehicle road departure accidents as well as head-on
  collisions due to temporary distraction. This system has limitations, since it
  highly depends on the number and quality of visible road markings, good lighting
  conditions, no fog or snow or any other extreme weather conditions.
- **Volkswagen**. The "Driver Fatigue Detection" system, by Volkswagen, automatically analyzes the driving characteristics and—if they indicate possible
  fatigue—recommends that the driver take a break [10]. The system continually

evaluates steering wheel movements along with other signals in the vehicle on motorways and others roads at speeds in excess of 65 km/h, and calculates a fatigue estimate. If fatigue is detected, the driver is warned by information in the multi-function display and an acoustic signal. The warning is repeated after 15 min if the driver has not taken a break.

3.2   Independent Products

In addition to driver alert technologies developed by auto manufacturers, similar systems are available to the owners of older vehicles through the aftermarket. Some aftermarket driver alert systems include:

- **EyeTracker:** This system was created by the Fraunhofer Institute for Digital Media Technology in Germany [2]. It consists of at least two cameras because stereoscopic vision is an essential part of the detection method. It is presented as a small modular system completely independent of the car being used. The employed tracking strategy allows for determining spatial position of the eyes and easy calculation of the direction of driver's gaze.
- **Anti Sleep Pilot:** This is the only system to date that combines subjective methods with vehicle-based methods in one system [6]. It consists of a small device that is easily mountable on the car's dashboard. It requires from a driver to take a questionnaire prior to the trip, which will create the driver's personal risk profile and prior fatigue status. Additionally, it monitors driving through various built-in sensors. The alertness level is constantly monitored by an alertness maintaining test that prompts the driver to respond to audiovisual cues from the device.
- **Seeing Machines DSS:** This is a product of Seeing Machines Ltd., specifically modified for use in vehicle systems. It uses a small, dashboard-mounted, camera for eye behavior tracking [1].
- **Takata SafeTrak:** This system by Takata corporation consists of a small video camera, which provides input to a sophisticated machine vision software in order to monitor the road ahead and warn drivers if they unintentionally leave their lane or if their driving pattern starts to indicate erratic behavior [7].
- **Nap Zapper:** This is an inexpensive and simple device, mounted over the driver's ear (it has the size of a typical external hearing aid) [5]. At its core lies an electronic position sensor that detects when the driver's head nods forward and sounds an audio alarm. This device might prove useful in certain situations such as long distance driving on monotonous, straight roads.

References

1. DSS. Eyetracker watches drivers' eyes for signs of drowsiness. online article, 2012.
2. F. I. for Digital Media Technology. Eyetracker watches drivers' eyes for signs of drowsiness. online article, 2010.
3. Ford. Ford driver alert. http://corporate.ford.com/microsites/sustainability-report-2012-13/vehicle-technologies-avoidance, 2012.
4. Mercedes-Benz. Attention assist: Drowsiness-detection system warns drivers to prevent them falling asleep momentarily. online article, 2008.
5. NapZapper. Nap zapper. http://www.napzapper.com/.
6. A. S. Pilot. Eyetracker watches drivers' eyes for signs of drowsiness. online article, 2012.
7. Takata. Safetrak 1++. http://www.safetrak.takata.com/ProductDetails.aspx, 2009.
8. Toyota. Lexus ls advanced active safety features. http://www.newcarnet.co.uk/lexus_news.html?id=5787, 2012.
9. Toyota. Toyota redesigns crown and introduces hybrid model. http://www.worldcarfans.com/10802192219/toyota-redesigns-crown--introduces-hybrid-model, 2012.
10. Volkswagen. Driver alert. http://www-nrd.nhtsa.dot.gov/pdf/esv/esv19/Other/Print, 2012.
11. Volvo. Volvo driver alert control and lane departure warning system. http://www.zercustoms.com/news/Volvo-Driver-Alert-Control-and-Lane-Departure-Warning.html, 2007.

Chapter 4
Research Aspects

This chapter presents an overview of the research aspects associated with the development of driver drowsiness detection (DDD) solutions. It summarizes relevant technologies, popular algorithms, and design challenges associated with such systems. It focuses particularly on vehicle-mounted solutions that perform noninvasive monitoring of the driver's head and face for behavioral signs of potential drowsiness, such as nodding, yawning, or blinking. Typically, systems based on this methodology use a video camera for image acquisition and rely on a combination of computer vision and machine learning techniques to detect events of interest, measure them, and make a decision on whether the driver may be drowsy or not. If the sequence of captured images and measured parameters (e.g., pattern of nodding or time lapsed in "closed eye state") suggest that the driver is drowsy, an action—such as sounding an alarm—might be warranted.

DDD systems based on visual input are specialized computer vision solutions, which capture successive video frames, process each frame, and make decisions based on the analysis of the processed information. After capturing each frame using an imaging sensor (Sect. 4.1), one or more feature detection and extraction algorithms (Sect. 4.2) are applied to the pixel data. Their goal is to detect the presence and location of critical portions of the image (e.g., head, face, and eyes), measure their properties, and encode the results into numerical representations, which can then be used as input by a machine learning classifier (Sect. 4.3) that makes decisions such as "drowsy or not-drowsy" based on the analyzed data.

In the remainder of the chapter we discuss selected imaging sensors, feature extraction algorithms, machine learning classifiers, and conclude by looking at challenges and constraints associated with this field of research and development.

© The Author(s) 2014
A. Čolić et al., *Driver Drowsiness Detection*, SpringerBriefs in Computer Science,
DOI 10.1007/978-3-319-11535-1_4

4.1   Imaging Sensors

The imaging sensors used in most DDD systems fall into one of these two categories, depending on the range of the electromagnetic spectrum in which they operate: (i) visible light ("conventional") cameras; or (ii) near infrared (NIR) cameras. The former can provide excellent resolution at relatively low cost, but depend on appropriate lighting conditions to operate satisfactorily. The latter can be used—often in addition to conventional cameras—to handle nighttime and other poor lighting situations.

4.1.1   Visible Light Cameras

The two most popular technologies for imaging sensors used in visible light cameras are either CCD (Charge-Coupled Device) and CMOS (Complementary Metal-Oxide Semiconductor). Both of the sensors perform essentially the same function, namely the conversion of light into electrical signals which can be further encoded, stored, processed, transmitted, and analyzed by specialized algorithms.

In a CCD sensor, every pixel's charge is transferred through a very limited number of output nodes (often just one) to be converted to voltage, buffered, and sent off-chip as an analog signal. An analog-to-digital converter turns each pixel's value into a digital value. CCDs use a special manufacturing process to create the ability to transport charge across the chip without distortion. This process leads to very high-quality sensors in terms of fidelity and light sensitivity.

In a CMOS sensor, each pixel has its own charge-to-voltage conversion, and the sensor often also includes amplifiers, noise-correction, and digitization circuits, so that the chip outputs digital bits. These other functions increase the design complexity and reduce the area available for light capture. With each pixel doing its own conversion, uniformity is lower, but it is also massively parallel, allowing high total bandwidth for high speed.

Both of these technologies have their advantages and disadvantages. The CCD technology is considered to have matured over time but the CMOS is slowly catching up with them. CCD sensors create high-quality, low noise and high resolution images. CMOS sensors are usually more susceptible to noise and their light sensitivity is lower then CCDs. In terms of power consumption, CMOS technology requires substantially less power. CMOS also leads as a cheaper to fabricate technology because CMOS chips can be fabricated on just about any standard silicon product line, which makes them fairly inexpensive.

Driver Drowsiness Detection systems need cameras that can produce high quality images with high resolution and low noise level which is so far the domain of the CCD cameras; on the other hand, the chosen imaging sensor should be cheap and battery efficient, which tilts the scale toward CMOS. The final decision will be a tradeoff among these pros and cons of each candidate technology.

4.1.2 Near Infrared (NIR) Cameras

One of the most common limitations of computer vision systems, in general, is their inability to perform consistently well across a wide range of operating conditions, e.g., when the lighting conditions are significantly different than the ones for which the system was designed and tested. In the case of vehicle-mounted solutions that rely on visual input, the ability to tolerate large variations in light intensity (from bright sunlight to nighttime driving on unlit roads) presents a formidable challenge. The solution for ensuring operability in low lighting conditions usually includes using a NIR camera as a sensor.

The term "near infrared" refers to a small portion of the much larger region called infrared (IR), located between the visible and microwave portions of the electromagnetic spectrum. NIR makes up the part of IR closest in wavelength to visible light and occupies the wavelengths between about 700 and 1,500 nm (0.7–1.5 μm). NIR is not to be confused with thermal infrared, which is on the opposite end of the infrared spectrum (wavelengths in the (8–15 μm) range) and measures radiant (emitted) heat. NIR cameras are available in either CCD or CMOS sensors, and they can provide monochrome or color images at their output.

DDD systems that use NIR cameras usually employ an additional source of NIR radiation, such as LEDs designed to emit radiation in NIR frequency band, to illuminate the object of interest and, in that way, amplify the input values for the camera. It is common to have the LEDs focus on the driver's eyes, because of the pupils' noticeable ability to reflect infrared, which leads to a quick and effective way to locate the position of the eyes [3, 6, 7, 14].

4.2 Feature Detection and Extraction

Generally speaking, any system designed to monitor the state of an object of interest over time must be capable of detecting that object, determining what state the object is in, and tracking its movements. In computer vision systems, the detection and tracking steps are based on extracting useful features from the pixel data and building models that represent the object of interest. In the specific case of DDD systems whose goal is to determine the drowsiness state of a driver by observing the driver's facial features, the focus is on the head, face, and eyes. Some of the most widely used facial features and corresponding feature extraction methods are described next.

Light Intensity Differentiation The grayscale representation of a face can be described as a collection of dark and bright areas, where usually the region of the eyes is much darker then the region of the nose and cheeks and the eyes are darker then the bridge of the nose. If we take each of these regions and describe them as a simple rectangle with bright or dark values inside, we are describing them in terms of Haar-like features [24]. Put simply, eyes and cheeks can be represented as two rectangles vertically adjacent to each other, while darker one is on top of the brighter one. And in the other case we would need three rectangles adjacent horizontally to each other, two dark ones for the eyes and one bright one for the nose in the middle. So the face can be represented with a different combination of dark and light rectangles. Algorithms using Haar-like features scan throughout the image, looking for best matches of rectangular patterns.

The most famous face detection algorithm in this category is the Viola-Jones algorithm [24]. It is based on exploiting perspective that a face (or any object, for that matter) can be represented as a collection of dark and bright regions as explained above. Haar-like features represent relationships between two different adjacent regions. Since there are many different regions on a human face and every region has a different relationship with different neighbor regions, the number of possible combinations is potentially huge. For a detection system to be efficient and fast it needs to rely on a subset of combinations, focusing on relationships between adjacent rectangle areas, which will be big enough to efficiently describe the object of interest. To determine what Haar-like features are significant and necessary in describing the object, a machine learning algorithm called Adaptive Boosting (or simply, AdaBoost) is used. The AdaBoost algorithm eliminates all small, irrelevant features and leaves just the set that is necessary. It has been shown that only two Haar-like features are enough to describe the human face. The first feature measures the difference in intensity between the region of the eyes and a region across the upper cheeks, which shows that eye region is often darker then the of the upper cheeks. The second feature compares the intensities in the eye regions to the intensity across the bridge of the nose. Again, eye regions are often darker then nose region. It was shown that these two are the most consistent features across big number of images. So if and area of interest shows to contain areas with such a relationship there is a good possibility that the area of interest contains a human face (Fig. 4.1).

In the driver drowsiness detection literature, there are many solutions which have adopted this feature extraction algorithm in their systems [4, 8, 14, 18, 26].

Skin Color Another popular method used for face detection purposes is the detection of regions of the image whose color properties are within the range of color tones associated with the human skin color [11]. Some researchers in the field of driver drowsiness detection systems have exploited the knowledge that skin colors' Red and Green components follow planar Gauss distribution which can be used as a search parameter for finding a face [9] while others are using the YCbCr color model for easier focus on the color of the face while eliminating the intensity component [23].

Texture Texture gives us information about the spatial arrangement of color or intensities in an image or selected region of an image. A human face can be seen as a composition of micro texture patterns. Eye regions usually contain more fine-grained texture than, for example, the cheeks. Every part of a human face can be described with its unique texture qualities. The most commonly used way of quantifying texture in this domain is by expressing it in terms of Local Binary

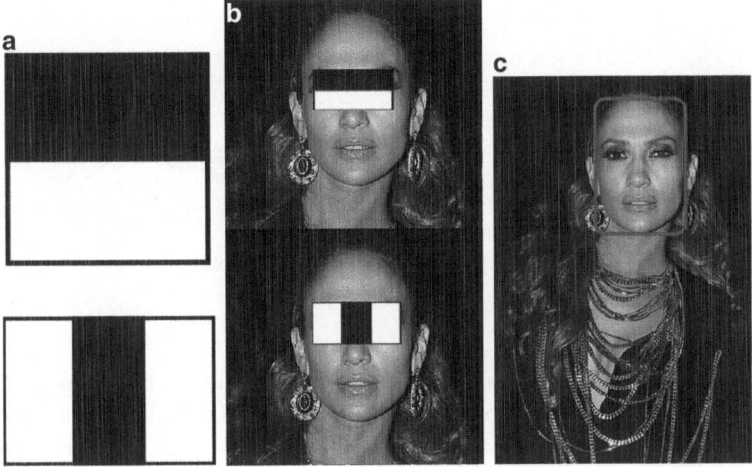

Fig. 4.1 Typical face detection steps based on Haar-like features. (**a**) Haar-like feature. (**b**) Applied on the candidate. (**c**) Face detected

Pattern (LBP) features. A face can be divided into subsections, each with its own unique texture quality. Algorithms can search for similar spacial relationships within the image to potentially locate the face or eyes [1, 11].

Local Binary Pattern (LBP) is a simple yet very efficient texture operator which labels the pixels of an image by thresholding the neighborhood of each pixel and considers the result as a binary number. Perhaps the most important property of the LBP operator in real-world applications is its robustness to monotonic grayscale changes caused, for example, by illumination variations. Another important property is its computational simplicity. The LBP operator is a powerful means for quantitative texture description of an object of interest. The LBP operator is based on the observation that two-dimensional surface textures can be described by two complementary measures: local spatial patterns and grayscale contrast. The basic idea is to form labels for the image pixels by thresholding the 3×3 neighborhood of each pixel with the center value and considering the result as a binary number. Take a pixel as center and threshold its neighbors against. If the intensity of the center pixel is greater or equal to its neighbor, then denote it with 1 or 0 if otherwise. We end up with a binary number for each pixel, for example 11001111. With 8 surrounding pixels you'll end up with 2^8 (i.e., 256) possible combinations, which are called LBP codes. Usually the area of interest is divided into groups of nonoverlapping 3×3 (pixel) neighborhoods. LBP codes have the ability to capture very fine grained details in an area of interest and have produced results that were able to compete with state of the art benchmarks for texture classification when the method was first applied to face recognition [1]. Soon after the operator was published, it was noted that a fixed neighborhood fails to encode details differing in scale. As a result, the operator was extended to use a variable neighborhood.

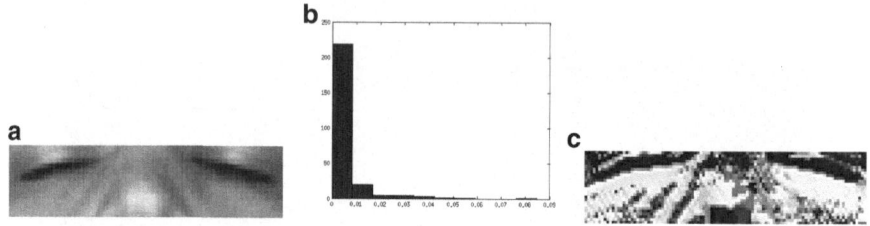

Fig. 4.2 Local Binary Pattern example. (**a**) Raw image. (**b**) LBP histogram. (**c**) LBP image

A face can be described as a composition of micro-patterns. Every micro-pattern has its own unique combination of textures which can be well described by LBP. Therefore, a face can be divided into subsections from which the LBP extraction can be performed (Fig. 4.2). LBP histograms can serve as an input vectors to a classifier.

Eigenfaces If we take any image of a human face and distort it so that the image becomes highly noisy, the distorted image will not look completely random and in spite of the differences between any two distorted images of any face there are same patterns which occur in them. Such patterns could be the presence of some objects (eyes, nose, mouth) as well as relative distances between these objects. These characteristic features are called *eigenfaces* in the facial recognition domain (Fig. 4.3). In general, we can treat any object from topological point of view as a sum of valleys and peaks and their relationships. If we take a face for example, eyes can be considered to be valleys compared to forehead, nose and cheeks. A commonly used algorithm for filtering images to emphasize on its topological structure is the 2D Gabor Function. It can enhance edge contours, as well as valleys and ridge contours of the image. A Gabor filter is a linear filter used for edge detection. The frequency and orientation representations of Gabor filters are similar to those of the human visual system, and they have been found to be particularly appropriate for texture representation and discrimination. In the spatial domain, a 2D Gabor filter is a Gaussian kernel function modulated by a sinusoidal plane wave. The Gabor filters are self-similar which means that all filters can be generated from one mother wavelet by dilation and rotation.

Infrared (IR) Sensitivity Among the features that are unique only to eyes is the fact that the eye's pupil reflects almost all of the incoming IR radiation, while the rest of the human body is absorbing it. This phenomenon can be easily detected and exploited for face/eye detection purposes in DDD systems equipped with the appropriate sensors [3, 6, 15]. In such cases, the reflection of IR light from the pupil produces a nicely shaped circle, which can be detected using the Circular Hough Transform [11].

Horizontal and Vertical Projection The summation of grayscale pixel values in every column/row in an image is called the vertical/horizontal projection. Summed values compared to each other can reveal local minima and maxima in an image

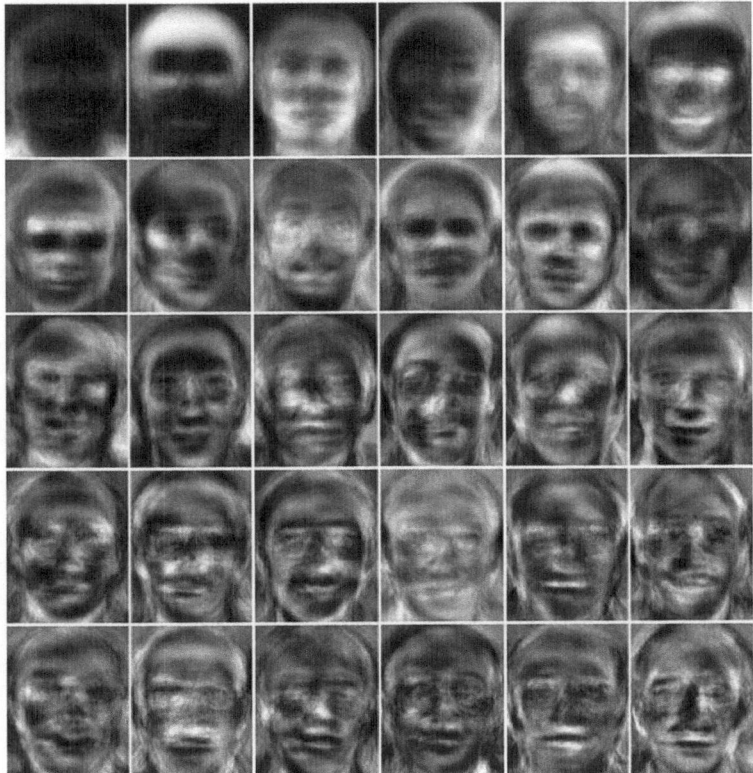

Fig. 4.3 Examples of eigenfaces

(Fig. 4.4). Every object usually contains a specific set of local minima and maxima that can be used as characteristic to describe that object, a feature that has been used in various research studies in the literature [6, 25].

Scale-Invariant Feature Transform (SIFT) SIFT is an algorithm in computer vision to detect and describe local features in images. The SIFT feature descriptor is invariant to uniform scaling, orientation, and partially invariant to affine distortion and illumination changes. Once it has been computed, an image is transformed into a large collection of feature vectors, each of which is invariant to image translation, scaling, and rotation, partially invariant to illumination changes and robust to local geometric distortion. These features share similar properties with neurons in inferior temporal cortex that are used for object recognition in primate vision. Key locations are defined as maxima and minima of the result of difference of Gaussian (DoG) function applied in scale space to a series of smoothed and re-sampled images. Low contrast candidate points and edge response points along an edge are discarded. Dominant orientations are assigned to localized key points. These steps ensure that the key points are more stable for matching and recognition. SIFT descriptors, robust

Fig. 4.4 Example of
horizontal projection

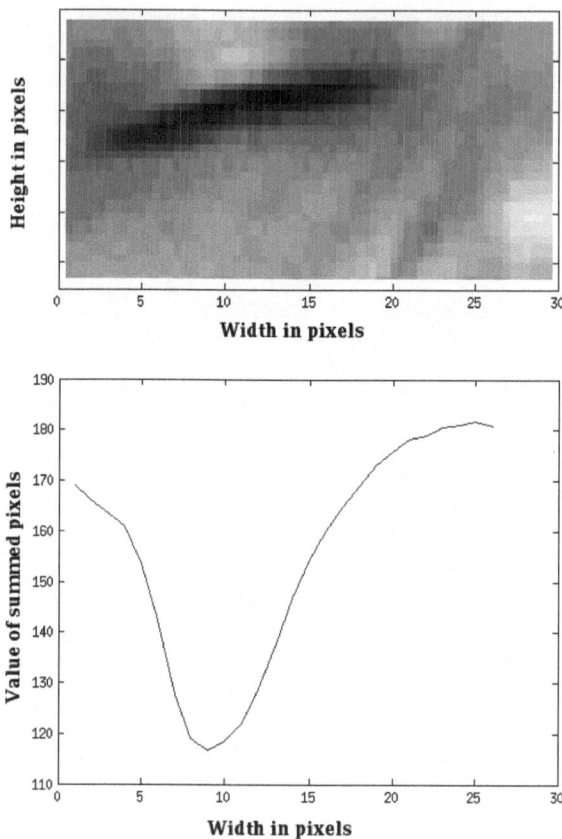

to local affine distortion, are then obtained by considering pixels around a radius of
the key location, blurring and re-sampling of local image orientation planes. Every
state of the object will produce unique set of SIFT features which is can be used to
distinguish them [11].

4.3   Machine Learning Classifiers

Once the contents of the significant portions of an image have been detected,
extracted, and encoded, the resulting representation is used as input for machine
learning techniques capable of distinguishing among two or more classes. In the
context of DDD systems, the problem fundamentally boils down to a two-class
classification problem, namely to tell whether the driver may be drowsy or not.

The most widely used classifiers in DDD systems are neural networks, AdaBoost,
and support vector machines (SVM).

Neural Networks This is a mathematical model inspired by biological neural networks. A neural network consists of an interconnected group of artificial neurons, and it processes information using a connectionist approach to computation. In most cases a neural network is an adaptive system, changing its structure during a learning phase. Neural networks are used for modeling complex relationships between inputs and outputs or to find patterns in data. This machine learning method is used widely in the object detection world because it provides: (a) generalization (small distortions can be handled easily); (b) expandability (learning a different set of objects will require hardly any change to the structure of the program); (c) the ability to represent multiple samples (a class of objects can easily be represented by multiple samples under multiple conditions); and (d) efficiency (once trained, the network determines in one single step to what class the object belongs). The downside of this method is that they require a large and diverse set of training examples, as well as demanding processing and storage resources. Small recognition systems, though, should benefit from all the advantages of using a neural network as a classifier [22].

Adaptive Boosting AdaBoost is an adaptive machine learning algorithm, in the sense that subsequent classifiers built are tweaked in favor of those instances misclassified by previous classifiers. AdaBoost generates and calls a new weak classifier in each of a series of rounds. For each call, a distribution of weights is updated that indicates the importance of the examples in the dataset for the classification. On each round, the weights of each incorrectly classified examples are increased, and the weights of each correctly classified example are decreased, so the new classifier focuses on the examples which have so far eluded correct classification. Even though AdaBoost can be sensitive to noisy data, its efficiency is what has drawn many researchers towards using it [4, 16].

SVM Support Vector Machines are based on the concept of decision planes that define decision boundaries (Fig. 4.5). A decision plane is one that separates between a set of objects having different class memberships. The basic SVM takes a set of input data and predicts, for each given input, which of two possible classes forms the output, making it a non-probabilistic binary linear classifier. Given a set of training examples, each marked as belonging to one of two categories, a SVM training algorithm builds a model that assigns new examples into one category or the other. A SVM model is a representation of the examples as points in space, mapped so that the examples of the separate categories are divided by a clear gap that is as wide as possible. New examples are then mapped into that same space and predicted to belong to a category based on which side of the gap they fall on. If the sets of objects can be classified into their respective groups by a line the SVM is linear. Most classification tasks, however, are not that simple, and often more complex structures are needed in order to make an optimal separation. Using different set of mathematical equations called *kernels*, SVM can try to rearrange the input data so that the gap between different classes is as wide as possible and the separation line can clearly be drawn between the classes. SVM is very powerful and easy to understand tool, which explains its popularity [13, 26].

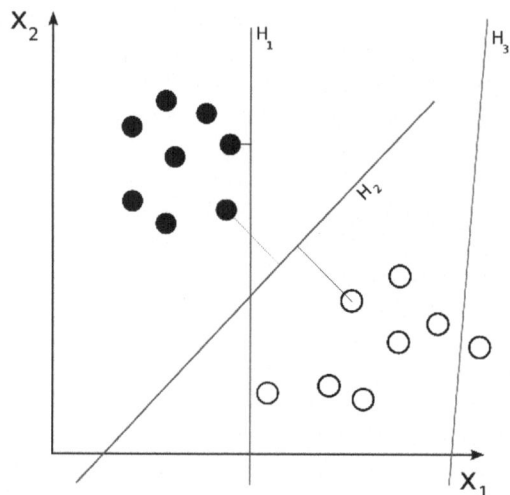

Fig. 4.5 Concept of a Support Vector Machine. Source: Wikimedia Commons

4.4   Challenges and Practical Aspects

DDD systems are complex pieces of engineering, which should perform reliably under a broad range of practical scenarios. In this section we summarize some of the challenges and practical issues involved in the design and development of successful DDD systems.

4.4.1   Data Collection

Due to the difficulty in collecting proper (electro-physiological, behavioral etc.) driver drowsiness data in a real world environment, researchers have resorted to safe and controlled simulated environments to carry out their experiments. The main advantages of using simulators include: experimental control, efficiency, low cost, safety, and ease of data collection [10, 19].

Driving simulators are being increasingly used for training drivers all over the world. Research has shown that driving simulators are proven to be excellent practical and effective educational tools to impart safe driving training techniques for all drivers. There are various types of driving simulators in use today, e.g., train simulator, bus simulator, car simulator, truck simulator etc. The most complex, such as the National Advanced Driving Simulator (Fig. 4.6), have a full-sized vehicle body, with six-axis movement and 360-degree visual displays.

On the other end of the range, there are simple desktop simulators such as the York Driving Simulator, which are often implemented using a computer monitor for

Fig. 4.6 National Advanced Driving Simulator

the visual display and a video game-type steering wheel and pedal input devices. These low cost simulators are used readily in the evaluation of basic and clinically oriented scientific questions [5, 12, 20, 21].

Some research teams are using automated vehicles to recreate simulator studies on a test track, enabling a more direct comparison between the simulator study and the real world [17]. One important limitation of using driving simulators also is that the drivers do not perceive any risk. The awareness of being immersed in a simulated environment might give a behavior which is different than that on an actual road [2]. However, the consensus among researchers is that driving simulators can create driving environments that are sufficiently similar to road experiments.

4.4.2 Performance Requirements

A successful DDD system must be fast, robust, reliable, nonintrusive and proactive.

The ultimate goal of such systems is to work in a real world, which means that the system should reach conclusive decisions about the state of the driver (and the need to issue an alert) in a timely manner. Failure to respond within a reasonable amount of time (a few seconds) may turn out to be catastrophic and opposite to the original goal of having these systems in the first place. Real-time performance is desired, but it might come at the cost of increased computing power, which would also increase battery consumption and the cost of the overall solution accordingly.

A DDD system has to be robust and should perform under various conditions, including severe weather, large variations in overall lighting, bumpy roads (and their impact on the quality of the acquired video frames), and noise, to mention but a few. Once again, there will be a point beyond which a system will ultimately stop working properly. The challenge is to bring this point as far away as possible from normal operating conditions, without sacrificing any other major aspect of the solution.

A DDD system must be reliable, since ultimately there are human lives at stake. It belongs to the categories of systems for which the cost of a false positive is significantly lower than the cost of a false negative. In other words, it is best to (occasionally) issue an alert when none was necessary (a false positive) than to miss a truly serious situation that might lead to an accident (a false negative).

A DDD system should be nonintrusive. Its setup and components should be used in a way that does not disturb normal driving. The driver's undivided attention has to be on the road and the situation ahead of the car. The driver should not be distracted by audio and visual distractions coming from the system. Moreover, the hardware portion of the system should be small and discreet and properly placed, so as to not occlude part of the driver's view. Moreover, physical interactions between the system and the driver should be kept to a minimum, basically providing a quick setup and calibration in the initialization phase, a friendly way to dismiss false alarms (if any), and very little else.

Finally, a DDD system has to be proactive. It has to be capable of attracting the driver's attention when necessary. Usually, a DDD system will use audio/visual cues to communicate warning/alert messages to the driver, reporting suspicion of drowsy behavior and trying to prevent a potentially dangerous situation. Care must be taken to avoid causing sudden erratic behavior or startling the driver due to a loud alarm, for example. Moreover, fallback provisions (e.g., applying the vehicle's brakes) might be implemented if it has become clear that the driver is not responding to the system's warnings.

References

1. T. Ahonen, A. Hadid, and M. Pietikäinen. Face recognition with local binary patterns. In *ECCV (1)*, pages 469–481, 2004.
2. F. Bella. Driver perception of roadside configurations on two-lane rural roads: Effects on speed and lateral placement. *Accident Analysis and Prevention*, 50(0):251–262, 2013.
3. L. Bergasa, J. Nuevo, M. Sotelo, R. Barea, and M. Lopez. Real-time system for monitoring driver vigilance. *Intelligent Transportation Systems, IEEE Transactions on*, 7(1):63–77, 2006.
4. E. Cheng, B. Kong, R. Hu, and F. Zheng. Eye state detection in facial image based on linear prediction error of wavelet coefficients. In *Robotics and Biomimetics, 2008. ROBIO 2008. IEEE International Conference on*, pages 1388–1392, 2009.
5. D. Dawson, C. J. van den Heuvel, K. J. Reid, S. N. Biggs, and S. D. Baulk. Chasing the silver bullet: Measuring driver fatigue using simple and complex tasks. *Accident analysis and prevention*, 40(1):396–402, 2008.
6. W. Dong and P. Qu. Eye state classification based on multi-feature fusion. In *Control and Decision Conference, 2009. CCDC '09. Chinese*, pages 231–234, 2009.
7. M. J. Flores, J. M. Armingol, and A. de la Escalera. Real-time warning system for driver drowsiness detection using visual information. *Journal of Intelligent and Robotic Systems*, 59(2):103–125, 2010.
8. T. Hong, H. Qin, and Q. Sun. An improved real time eye state identification system in driver drowsiness detection. In *Control and Automation, 2007. ICCA 2007. IEEE International Conference on*, pages 1449–1453, 2007.

9. C. Jiangwei, J. Lisheng, G. Lie, G. Keyou, and W. Rongben. Driver's eye state detecting method design based on eye geometry feature. In *Intelligent Vehicles Symposium, 2004 IEEE*, pages 357–362, 2004.

10. P. Konstantopoulos, P. Chapman, and D. Crundall. Driver's visual attention as a function of driving experience and visibility. using a driving simulator to explore drivers' eye movements in day, night and rain driving. *Accident Analysis and Prevention*, 42(3):827–834, 2010.

11. A. Lenskiy and J.-S. Lee. Driver's eye blinking detection using novel color and texture segmentation algorithms. *International Journal of Control, Automation and Systems*, 10(2):317–327, 2012.

12. Z. Li and P. Milgram. An investigation of the potential to influence braking behaviour through manipulation of optical looming cues in a simulated driving task. *Proceedings of the Human Factors and Ergonomics Society Annual Meeting*, 49(17):1540–1544, 2005.

13. C.-C. Lien and P.-R. Lin. Drowsiness recognition using the Least Correlated LBPH. In *Intelligent Information Hiding and Multimedia Signal Processing (IIH-MSP), 2012 Eighth International Conference on*, pages 158–161, 2012.

14. A. Liu, Z. Li, L. Wang, and Y. Zhao. A practical driver fatigue detection algorithm based on eye state. In *Microelectronics and Electronics (PrimeAsia), 2010 Asia Pacific Conference on Postgraduate Research in*, pages 235–238, 2010.

15. D. Liu, P. Sun, Y. Xiao, and Y. Yin. Drowsiness detection based on eyelid movement. In *Education Technology and Computer Science (ETCS), 2010 Second International Workshop on*, volume 2, pages 49–52, 2010.

16. Z. Liu and H. Ai. Automatic eye state recognition and closed-eye photo correction. In *Pattern Recognition, 2008. ICPR 2008. 19th International Conference on*, pages 1–4, 2008.

17. W. Nic. Program develops new test track capability. The Sensor Newsletter, 2004.

18. C. Qingzhang, W. Wenfu, and C. Yuqin. Research on eye-state based monitoring for drivers' dozing. *Intelligent Information Technology Applications, 2007 Workshop on*, 1:373–376, 2009.

19. F. Rosey, S.-M. Auberlet, O. Moisan, and G. Dupré. Impact of narrower lane width: Comparison between fixed-base simulator and real data. *Transportation Research Record: Journal of the Transportation Research Board*, 2138(1):112–119, 2009.

20. J. Telner. *The Effects of Linguistic Fluency on Performance in a Simulated Cellular Telephone and Driving Situation*. Canadian theses. York University (Canada), 2008.

21. J. A. Telner, D. L. Wiesenthal, and E. Bialystok. Video gamer advantages in a cellular telephone and driving task. *Proceedings of the Human Factors and Ergonomic Society annual meeting*, 53(23):1748–1752, 2009.

22. Y.-l. Tian, T. Kanade, and J. F. Cohn. Eye-state action unit detection by Gabor Wavelets. In *Proceedings of the Third International Conference on Advances in Multimodal Interfaces*, ICMI '00, pages 143–150, London, UK, UK, 2000. Springer-Verlag.

23. Z. Tian and H. Qin. Real-time driver's eye state detection. In *Vehicular Electronics and Safety, 2005. IEEE International Conference on*, pages 285–289, 2005.

24. P. Viola and M. Jones. Robust real-time object detection. In *International Journal of Computer Vision*, 2001.

25. F. Wang, M. Zhou, and B. Zhu. A novel feature based rapid eye state detection method. In *Robotics and Biomimetics (ROBIO), 2009 IEEE International Conference on*, pages 1236–1240, 2009.

26. Y.-S. Wu, T.-W. Lee, Q.-Z. Wu, and H.-S. Liu. An eye state recognition method for drowsiness detection. In *Vehicular Technology Conference (VTC 2010-Spring), 2010 IEEE 71st*, pages 1–5, 2010.

Chapter 5
Examples

This chapter provides examples of recent research work on driver drowsiness detection solutions. The systems and methods discussed in this chapter complement the commercial solutions surveyed in Chap. 3. Most of the methods described below have been developed in the context of academic research and focus on behavioral aspects, such as nodding, blinking, and yawning. The chapter is divided into two main sections: Sect. 5.1 covers selected recent work by researchers in the field, whereas Sect. 5.2 presents highlights of the authors' ongoing work on the topic.

5.1 Selected Recent Work

There have been many recent efforts in the field of driver drowsiness detection using behavioral methods. As explained in Chap. 2, such methods are usually focused on monitoring the driver's facial expressions and recognizing patterns that might describe the driver's internal state. Visual clues that can be monitored for determining driver's sleep deprivation level include: sudden variations in head pose (presumably associated with nodding), frequent yawning, rapid blinking or prolonged eye closure. A driver's facial expressions and head pose can be monitored using camera sensors and an array of image processing and computer vision algorithms, e.g., face detection, head pose estimation, and feature tracking. In this section, we highlight prominent examples of recent work, classified into three categories: head pose estimation, yawning, and eye state estimation.

© The Author(s) 2014
A. Čolić et al., *Driver Drowsiness Detection*, SpringerBriefs in Computer Science,
DOI 10.1007/978-3-319-11535-1__5

5.1.1   Head Pose Estimation

A driver's head pose can provide significant amounts of information regarding the driver's internal state, level of attention and potential sleep deprivation.

The work by Zhang et al. proposes that monitoring driver's head pose and orientation can give enough clues to predict the driver's intent [21]. In order to determine the drivers' head pose, the driver's face has to be detected first. This is a typical primary step in any behavioral methodology based on monitoring a subject's face. The face detection algorithm proposed by Viola and Jones [18] has become a reference upon which other face detection methods can be built. Zhang et al. trained three classifiers (focused on horizontal rotation of the driver's head) in order to successfully detect front-facing, left-facing and right-facing faces. The way to determine the head's pose and orientation is by analyzing isophote features [8] of the driver's head. The isophote properties can capture important information about the face, such as direction, orientation and curvature. Two histograms are obtained from the isophote features: a histogram of direction and a histogram of curvature. The histograms' bin counts serve as the input data to a K-Nearest Neighbor (KNN) classifier [1] that will determine where the driver's head is facing at, relative to the camera.

Chutorian and Trivedi [13] created a three-part system capable of performing in real-time (i.e, at 30 frames per second) that can detect the driver's head, provide initial head pose estimation and continuously track the head's position and orientation. Similarly to the previously explained work, face detection is the first step of the system's architecture. Three Adaboost cascades are created to encompass left-facing, front-facing and right-facing faces in relation to the recording camera since they are the most commonly occurring poses of driver's head. Once successfully detected, facial region features are expressed as a localized gradient orientation (LGO) histogram [11] which has been shown to be invariant to image's scale and rotation as well as robust in relation to variations in illumination and noise. The LGO histogram is used as an input to a Support Vector Regression classifier [4], that can provide the driver's current head pose. One of the most interesting aspects of their work is that it is leaning on the use of augmented reality, by using a virtual environment that simulates the view space of the real camera [12].

5.1.2   Yawning

The capacity to estimate whether a driver is yawning and inferring, based on the frequency of yawning, whether he or she may be too drowsy to drive constitutes a challenging research problem. The ability to detect yawning state from input captured by a camera requires detecting features and learning states based on the relative position and state of the mouth and eyes. In recent years, several researchers have been working on the topic; two of those efforts are briefly summarized below.

Smith, Shah, and da Vitoria Lobo [16] proposed a fully automatic system, capable of multiple feature detections (among which is yawning), combating partial occlusions (like eye or mouth). In order to detect the driver's head the authors resorted to 2-part approach that first detects lips using specific lip color predicates in combination with mouth corner detection, followed by eye detection based on locating pair of non-skin-color regions above the previously detected lip region. Once those three anchors have been established, the head position and dimensions can be calculated. In order to determine the driver's attention, eye gaze is used as a main point. It is calculated geometrically by using two parallel eye gaze rays and their relationship to dashboard. To strengthen the attention level gained from reconstructing the gaze direction of a driver, additional aspects are tracked, e.g. yawning, which is determined by monitoring lip corners direction change as well as lip corner color change.

The proposed approach consists of eight main steps, as follows [16]: (1) automatically initialize lips and eyes using color predicates and connected components; (2) track lip corners using dark line between lips and color predicate even through large mouth movement like yawning; (3) track eyes using affine motion and color predicates; (4) construct a bounding box of the head; (5) determine rotation using distances between eye and lip feature points and sides of the face; (6) determine eye blinking and eye closing using the number and intensity of pixels in the eye region; (7) reconstruct 3-D gaze; and (8) determine driver visual attention level using all acquired information.

More recently, work by Saradadevi and Bajaj [15] focuses more specifically on yawning analysis. In order to detect the mouth, a Haar-like-feature-based classifier is trained. Once the mouth is successfully detected, its state is determined by using a Support Vector Machine classifier [3] which is trained to distinguish between two different sets of data: open mouth state (yawning) and closed mouth state. The authors performed training of SVM by providing about 20 yawning images and more than 1,000 regular images along with few videos from which 10 yawning images and 10 regular images are added to the training set. The videos are than used as testing sequences. A correct detection rate of over 80 % is achieved.

5.1.3   Eye State Estimation

The most commonly used visual clue for determining a driver's drowsiness level is state of the eyes. Several recent approaches to solve this problem are summarized next.

Liu et al. [10] decided to explore the advantages of infrared camera in order to monitor driver's eyes. Some of the infrared sensors' main advantages are the ability to operate during nighttime and their lower sensitivity to light changes. The Viola-Jones algorithm is used once again to initially detect the driver's face and eyes. If the eyes are successfully located, the eye regions are extracted for further processing. The algorithm can detect eye corners from given eye regions and—with given geometrical and statistical restrictions—the movement of the eyelids can be detected and used as a measure of eye closeness. The frequency of blinking is used as a measurement of how fatigued is the driver. The algorithm can track eyes in higher speeds after initial eye detection and is gender independent as well as resilient towards low levels of lighting.

The work by Wu et al. [20] also determines driver's drowsiness by monitoring state of the eyes of a driver. Their detection process is divided into three stages: (i) initial face detection based on classification of Haar-like features using the AdaBoost method; (ii) eye detection by SVM classification of eye candidates acquired by applying radial-symmetry transformation to the detected face from the previous stage; and (iii) extraction of local binary pattern (LBP) feature out of left eye candidate, which can be used to train the SVM classifier to distinguish between open eye state and closed eye state. The LBP of an eye can be thought of as a simplified texture representation of it. Both closed- and open-eye LBPs are distinguishable by two-state classifiers such as the SVM.

Tian and Qin [17] propose that combining several basic image processing algorithms can increase the performance of eye state detection system and bring it closer to real time performance. Moreover, two different methodologies are proposed for daytime and nighttime detection. In order to detect the driver's face during daytime, a combination of skin color matching with vertical projection is performed. This color matching will not work during night, therefore vertical projection is performed on the cropped face region acquired after adjusting image intensity to have uniform background. For locating the eyes, horizontal projection is applied on the previously detected face. The eye region is then converted to a binary image in order to emphasize the edges of the eyes. The converted image is processed through a complexity function, which provides an estimate of its complexity level: an image containing open eyes has more complex contours than another image containing closed eyes. The difference in complexity level can be used to distinguish between those two states.

In a follow-up work [5], Hong, Qin, and Sun introduced a few modifications to their original methodology. To increase success rate of face detection, an optimized Haar-like feature approach is used, due to its better detection rate and ability to reduce the number of false positives. An AdaBoost classifier is fed with both the results of applying a Canny edge detector to the image as well as the original image, resulting in increased face detection performance. An additional change that consequently provides better results in the eye detection state is that the detected face image is modified to eliminate the unwanted area about the head that can skew the results of horizontal projection. Additionally, smoothing part of the horizontal projection curve is eliminated, thereby increasing the speed of the algorithm. A complexity function is adopted to be able to compensate for environmental changes. Combined, all the optimization changes have increased the speed of the overall system to approach real-time performance.

Wang et al. [19] addresses the eye state detection problem by extracting discriminative features of the eye with unique intensity spatial correlation, such as the color correlogram [6], and using a reliable machine learning classification method (e.g., AdaBoost) to distinguish between open and closed eye states.

Several papers recognize the complexity of building the whole driver's drowsiness detection system and in return only focus on significant modules of the system. One example of such type of effort is a recent paper by Qin, Liu and Hong [14]. They strictly focus on eye state detection and identification while assuming that other modules, such as face and eye detection, are given. They propose building an eye model based on the Embedded Hidden Markov Model (EHMM) using color frequency features of images containing closed and open eyes extracted by applying two-dimensional Discrete Cosine Transformation (2-D DCT) on them. The low frequency coefficients are used to generate EHMM observation vectors that are then used to train the EHMM model of an eye.

Lien and Lin [9] follow the most commonly used approach of face and eye detection, feature extraction and eye state analysis based on different feature set for different eye state. In this paper they propose the computation of least correlated local binary patterns (LBP), which are used to create highly discriminate image features that can be used for robust eye state recognition. An additional novelty of the proposed method is the use of independent component analysis (ICA) in order to derive statistically independent and low dimensional feature vectors. The feature vectors are used as classification data for an SVM classifier, which provides information about the current eye state. This information is used to determine the frequency of blinking, which is then used to determine the state of the driver.

Lenskiy and Lee [7] propose a sophisticated system that monitors and measures the frequency of blinking as well as the duration of the eye being closed. In order to detect the eyes, a skin color segmentation algorithm with facial feature segmentation algorithm is used. For skin color segmentation, a neural network is trained by using RGB skin color histogram. Different facial regions, such as eyes, cheeks, nose, mouth etc. can be considered as different texture regions which can be used to sub-segment given skin model regions of interest. Each segment is filtered additionally to create SURF features that are used to estimate each class's probability density function (PDF). The segmented eye region is filtered with Circular Hough transform in order to locate iris candidates, i.e., the location of the driver's eyes. To track the eyes over an extended period of time, Kalman filtering is used.

5.2   Our Work

This section describes the requirements, constraints, basic architecture, and selected algorithms associated with a driver drowsiness detection system currently being developed by the authors. It consists of four stages:

1. System Initialization—Preparation
2. Regular Stage—Eye Tracking with Eye-State Analysis
3. Warning Stage—Nod Analysis
4. Alert Stage

Our approach follows a behavioral methodology by performing a non-invasive monitoring of external cues describing drivers level of drowsiness. We look at this complex problem from a systems' engineering point of view: how to go from a proof of concept prototype to a stable software framework that can provide solid basis for future research in this field.

5.2.1   System Initialization: Preparation

The initialization stage consists of analyzing the environment and optimizing some parameters for best performance. Our current prototype uses the camera capabilities of an Android-based smartphone device in order to observe the driver. The smartphone should be positioned as to enable appropriate distance and proper viewing angle between driver and camera. Moreover, the lighting conditions must be adequate (above a minimum threshold) and any potential occlusions of the camera view by the vehicle's internal components should be avoided.

Our system extracts user-specific features during the initialization stage. Those features include: skin color, head position and eye features. Once these features have been extracted, the process of localization of key components (head and eyes) takes place.

We use the Viola-Jones face/eyes detection algorithm [18], due to its speed and simplicity. The algorithm performs well if the user is facing the camera but the performance deteriorates fast as users gaze moves further away from the camera. Initial tests have shown that algorithm performs within the satisfactory boundaries both in terms of quality and speed. Typical limitations are shown in Figs. 5.1 and 5.2.

Tests have shown that face detection rate is high as long as the driver's gaze does not deviate more than 30 degrees relative to the camera. Conveniently, this allows for the positioning of the phone around the dashboard area of the car which is generally most commonly used place for positioning phone device. This position gives us a clear line of sight of a driver without the steering wheel occluding the view.

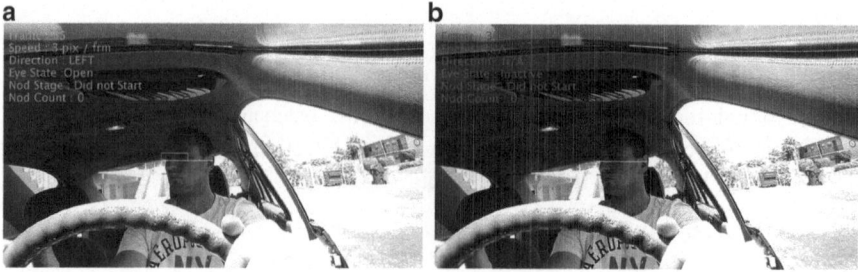

Fig. 5.1 Eye detection algorithm: limitations due to horizontal angle change. (**a**) Head rotating to the right—eyes still located properly. (**b**) Head rotating to the right—eyes lost in the following frame

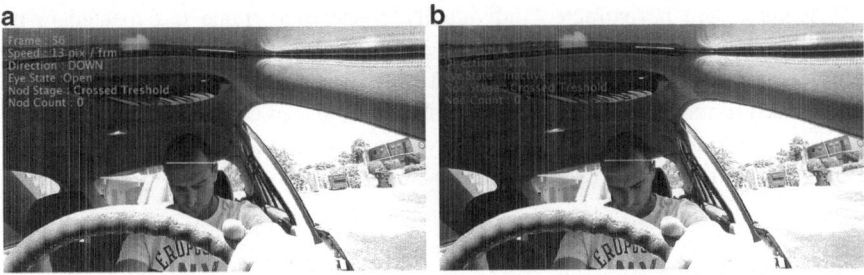

Fig. 5.2 Eye detection algorithm: limitations due to vertical angle change. (**a**) Head tilting forward—eyes still located properly. (**b**) Head tilting forward—eyes lost in the following frame

Fig. 5.3 Successful initial face and eyes detection

After proper positioning of the cameraphone, the main detection algorithm will locate the drivers face and consecutively drivers eyes. Figure 5.3 shows typical successful initial face and eyes detection.

In certain circumstances, when the phone position is off or the lighting conditions are significantly brighter or darker then normal, the system might not be able to initially locate face and eyes of the driver. In those cases, additional drivers help might be requested to manually extrapolate locations of key components. Driver will be exposed to very simple user interface where he will point towards location of his/her face by simply touching the area of the screen where face is located. He/she might also be required to keep their eyes closed and consequently open for certain duration of time in order to allow system to learn how to distinguish between those two states, a process that is explained in more detail in section "Eye Model Analysis".

Once all the required information has been acquired, the extraction of key features begins. This process takes a few seconds, during which each camera frame key features will be extracted individually. Since each frame is expected to be slightly different than the previous frame, our algorithm ensures that the built model will only include the unique qualities that were constant and consistent throughout all the used frames; all of the differences should be discarded as noise. Building this model helps us know what to specifically search for in the future frames, thereby significantly increasing the speed and robustness of the system.

Skin Color Feature Analysis

The idea of extracting skin color features of the drivers face is to create a user-specific skin model that can be used as alternative to or as complimentary face/eye detection and tracking method.

According to [2], the chroma components for human skin color using a YCbCr color model fall into the following ranges:

- Cb Range: 77–127
- Cr Range: 133–173

This range is purposefully created too broad and too general in order to encompass as many skin variations as possible. However, such a broad range does not compensate for illumination variation and also introduces a large number of false positives, Fig. 5.4a clearly shows that—using only these ranges—even though the face is successfully located, a large number of incorrect detections (e.g. in the t-shirt area) appeared in the result as well.

Our system overcomes this limitation by extracting the chroma values from the (previously detected) face pixels and producing a more accurate, user-centric range for chroma values. This process is computationally inexpensive but can significantly reduce the number of false positives, as shown in Fig. 5.4b.

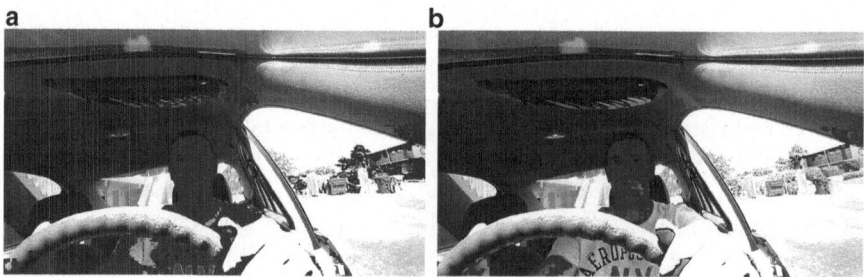

Fig. 5.4 Chroma-based skin detection comparison. (**a**) Generalized skin color chroma range. (**b**) User-specific skin color chroma range

Eye Model Analysis

Our system should be capable of reliably distinguishing between open and closed eyes. For that purpose, a Support Vector Machine classifier [3] was chosen. During the training stage, the classifier is fed with examples consisting of grayscale images of equal size that were cropped from frames used in the initialization stage, so as to contain only the (open or closed) eyes portion of the frame.

Head Position Analysis

Our prototype uses two main factors to determine if the driver is in a state that may require issuing a warning: (i) the duration of the driver's "closed eyes" state; and (ii) the detection of a characteristic type of nodding while the eyes are closed. We are interested in the type of nodding associated with dozing, which typically consists of a rapid vertical head drop with slow recovery back up. During the initialization stage, when the system interacts briefly with the driver for the sake of initial calibration, an analysis of the relative location of the driver's head within the frame allows the calculation of all the necessary parameters for correct functioning of the nod tracking method. Those parameters are used to create two thresholds. The nod tracking method will be based on driver's head's relative position compared to those two thresholds. In rested state, the driver keeps his/hers head in a fairly stationary position, above the upper threshold. The lower threshold can be determined by exploiting physical properties of a human body. Stretchability of a human neck are know as well as radius of motion of human head. It can be determined how much can head physically lean forward while nodding. Lower threshold can be statistically determined as a value beneath which we can claim that head nodded with high degree of certainty.

5.2.2   Regular Stage: Eye Tracking with Eye-State Analysis

At the end of the initialization stage, our system has successfully created the skin color model, the eye state model, and the head position model for the current driver. It is now ready to start actively tracking the driver's eyes and monitoring the driver's drowsiness level.

If the eyes are properly located in the initialization stage, tracking eye position through subsequent frames is a relatively straightforward task. In the current prototype, the tracking area will be dynamically defined based on the speed and direction of eye movement in previous frames. Basically, we apply the detection method based on the Viola-Jones algorithm to a candidate area where the eyes are expected to be found in subsequent frames. Since this corresponds to a small region of the overall frame, tracking is significantly faster compared to initial detection.

Additionally, in cases where the eyes are occluded in the subsequent frame, e.g. when the driver's head tilts forward during nodding, we use a skin color-based localization method to confirm that the face is still where it is expected to be, even though the eyes are occluded.

Once the eyes are successfully tracked in a given frame, the pixels containing only the eyes' region are cropped, converted to grayscale, and fed to the SVM classifier, which will determine the current state of the eyes: open or closed.

5.2.3   Warning Stage: Nod Analysis

The precondition for reaching the warning state is that either the driver keeps his or her eyes closed for prolonged amount of time or that specific head movement that can be classified as nodding started to happen. In our prototype, every time closed eyes are detected at a given point of time, timers will be activated to determine the duration of that state. Based on those timers, the system tries to determine if the driver is blinking or something else is happening. If the timer exceeds the duration of time considered to be safe to keep eyes closed while driving, the system switches to the warning stage. Once in the warning stage, the eyes continue to be tracked in the same manner as in the regular stage. The biggest difference is that the eye location and eye state are monitored more closely in order to detect if prolonged state of closed eyes continues or if a driver starts (or continues) to nod. If the behavior persists, it would mean that it is time to switch to final stage and alert the driver of the potential danger. If, on the other hand, the eyes become open at any time while the system is in a warning stage, that is used as a signal to return system into regular tracking stage and reset all the counters.

Head Position Monitoring

Sudden, sharp drop of the driver's head followed by slow recovery back up to the normal position might indicate that the driver is nodding and could be showing signs of sleepiness. In general, the position of a driver's head while driving feeling rested is usually above the upper threshold that system extrapolated in the initialization stage and does not change significantly over time (Fig. 5.5).

When the eyes start to move vertically down and their position crosses the upper threshold, our system considers that to be the potential beginning of a nodding sequence (Fig. 5.6a). If the head continues to vertically drop, portrayed with continuous downward movement of the eyes, eventually the lower threshold will be crossed (Fig. 5.6b). If true nodding occurrence is detected, crossing upper and lower thresholds should happen rather quickly, while recovering back up is usually a much slower process (Fig. 5.6c, d).

Fig. 5.5 Nod Stages: eyes above upper threshold

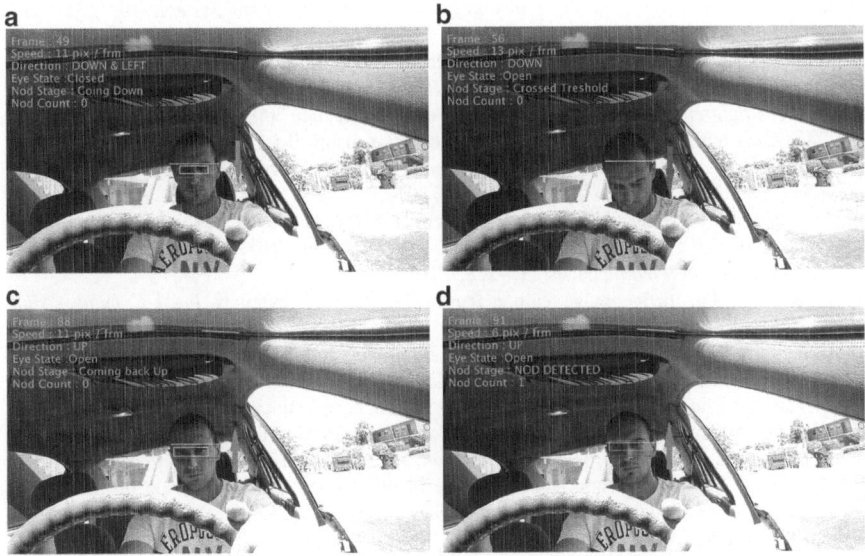

Fig. 5.6 Nodding detection method and its stages. (**a**) Head tilting down—eyes beneath the upper threshold. (**b**) Head tilting down—eyes beneath the lower threshold. (**c**) Head recovering up—eyes above lower threshold. Head recovering up—eyes above upper threshold: Nod is complete

5.2.4 Alert Stage

If the eyes are kept closed for exceedingly long periods of time and/or if the system detects that the driver has started nodding, it is time to alert the driver that his safety is in danger. This is accomplished in the current prototype by combining a high-pitch audio alert with a bright, colorful, visual warning on the smartphone's screen.

References

1. C. M. Bishop. *Pattern Recognition and Machine Learning (Information Science and Statistics)*. Springer-Verlag New York, Inc., Secaucus, NJ, USA, 2006.
2. D. Chai and K. N. Ngan. Face segmentation using skin-color map in videophone applications. *IEEE Trans. Cir. and Sys. for Video Technol.*, 9(4):551–564, June 1999.
3. C. Cortes and V. Vapnik. Support-vector networks. *Machine Learning*, 20(3):273–297, 1995.
4. H. Drucker, C. J. C. Burges, L. Kaufman, A. J. Smola, and V. Vapnik. Support vector regression machines. In *NIPS*, pages 155–161, 1996.
5. T. Hong, H. Qin, and Q. Sun. An improved real time eye state identification system in driver drowsiness detection. In *Control and Automation, 2007. ICCA 2007. IEEE International Conference on*, pages 1449–1453, 2007.
6. J. Huang, S. R. Kumar, M. Mitra, W.-J. Zhu, and R. Zabih. Image indexing using color correlograms. In *Proceedings of the 1997 Conference on Computer Vision and Pattern Recognition (CVPR '97)*, CVPR '97, pages 762–, Washington, DC, USA, 1997. IEEE Computer Society.
7. A. Lenskiy and J.-S. Lee. Driver's eye blinking detection using novel color and texture segmentation algorithms. *International Journal of Control, Automation and Systems*, 10(2):317–327, 2012.
8. J. Lichtenauer, E. Hendriks, and M. Reinders. Isophote properties as features for object detection. In *Computer Vision and Pattern Recognition, 2005. CVPR 2005. IEEE Computer Society Conference on*, volume 2, pages 649–654 vol. 2, June 2005.
9. C.-C. Lien and P.-R. Lin. Drowsiness recognition using the Least Correlated LBPH. In *Intelligent Information Hiding and Multimedia Signal Processing (IIH-MSP), 2012 Eighth International Conference on*, pages 158–161, 2012.
10. A. Liu, Z. Li, L. Wang, and Y. Zhao. A practical driver fatigue detection algorithm based on eye state. In *Microelectronics and Electronics (PrimeAsia), 2010 Asia Pacific Conference on Postgraduate Research in*, pages 235–238, 2010.
11. D. G. Lowe. Distinctive image features from scale-invariant keypoints. *Int. J. Comput. Vision*, 60(2):91–110, Nov. 2004.
12. E. Murphy-Chutorian and M. M. Trivedi. 3D tracking and dynamic analysis of human head movements and attentional targets. In *ICDSC*, pages 1–8. IEEE, 2008.
13. E. Murphy-Chutorian and M. M. Trivedi. Head pose estimation and augmented reality tracking: An integrated system and evaluation for monitoring driver awareness. *Intelligent Transportation Systems, IEEE Transactions on*, 11(2):300–311, 2010.
14. H. Qin, J. Liu, and T. Hong. An eye state identification method based on the Embedded Hidden Markov Model. In *Vehicular Electronics and Safety (ICVES), 2012 IEEE International Conference on*, pages 255–260, 2012.
15. M. Saradadevi and P. Bajaj. Driver fatigue detection using Mouth and Yawning analysis. *International Journal of Computer Science and Network Security*, 8(6):183–188, 2008.
16. P. Smith, M. Shah, and N. da Vitoria Lobo. Determining driver visual attention with one camera. *Intelligent Transportation Systems, IEEE Transactions on*, 4(4):205–218, 2003.
17. Z. Tian and H. Qin. Real-time driver's eye state detection. In *Vehicular Electronics and Safety, 2005. IEEE International Conference on*, pages 285–289, 2005.
18. P. Viola and M. Jones. Robust real-time object detection. *International Journal of Computer Vision*, 57(2):137–154, 2002.
19. H. Wang, L. Zhou, and Y. Ying. A novel approach for real time eye state detection in fatigue awareness system. In *Robotics Automation and Mechatronics (RAM), 2010 IEEE Conference on*, pages 528–532, 2010.
20. Y.-S. Wu, T.-W. Lee, Q.-Z. Wu, and H.-S. Liu. An eye state recognition method for drowsiness detection. In *Vehicular Technology Conference (VTC 2010-Spring), 2010 IEEE 71st*, pages 1–5, 2010.
21. X. Zhang, N. Zheng, F. Mu, and Y. He. Head pose estimation using isophote features for driver assistance systems. In *Intelligent Vehicles Symposium, 2009 IEEE*, pages 568–572, 2009.